EVERYBODY CAN
TRAIN
THEIR OWN DOG

THE ESSENTIALS OF DOG TRAINING

Title page: *Author Angela White with dogs belonging to the pupils of one of her summer camps.*

Distributed in the UNITED STATES by T.F.H. Publications, Inc., One T.F.H. Plaza, Neptune City, NJ 07753; in CANADA to the Pet Trade by H & L Pet Supplies Inc., 27 Kingston Crescent, Kitchener, Ontario N2B 2T6; Rolf C. Hagen Ltd., 3225 Sartelon Street, Montreal 382 Quebec; in CANADA to the Book Trade by Macmillan of Canada (A Division of Canada Publishing Corporation), 164 Commander Boulevard, Agincourt, Ontario M1S 3C7; in ENGLAND by T.F.H. Publications, PO Box 15, Waterlooville PO7 6BQ; in AUSTRALIA AND THE SOUTH PACIFIC by T.F.H. (Australia) Pty. Ltd., Box 149, Brookvale 2100 N.S.W., Australia; in NEW ZEALAND by Ross Haines & Son, Ltd., 82 D Elizabeth Knox Place, Panmure, Auckland, New Zealand; in the PHILIPPINES by Bio-Research, 5 Lippay Street, San Lorenzo Village, Makati, Rizal; in SOUTH AFRICA by Multipet Pty. Ltd., P.O. Box 35347, Northway, 4065, South Africa. Published by T.F.H. Publications, Inc. Manufactured in the United States of America by T.F.H. Publications, Inc.

EVERYBODY CAN
TRAIN
THEIR OWN DOG

THE ESSENTIALS OF DOG TRAINING

Angela White

Dedication

To Mum—who through passive training and positive shaping moulded me into an individual who, with a little motivation, can achieve a lifetime of ambitions.

CONTENTS

Preface 6
Acknowledgements 7
About the Author 9
Introduction: Understanding
  the Doggy Mind 11
Adolescence: 15
Aggression 17
Appetite 23
Barking 24
Bedtime 29
Biting 31
Breeding 34
Cages/Crates 38
Chasing 40
Chewing 43
Children and Dogs 48
Classes and Clubs 50
Compulsive Behaviour 53
Coprophagy 54
Crossing the Road 55
Diet 57
Digging 59
Disabilities 61
Distraction Training 64
Dominance 68
Down 71
Eating Grass 76
Energy 77
Equipment 82
Excitement 87
Exercise 89
Fearfulness 92
Feeding 95
Fighting 97
Grooming 100
Guarding 103
Housetraining 104
Howling 108
Hyperactivity 109
Inoculation 112
Intelligence 113
Jealousy 118
Jumping Up 119
Kennels 122
Leave on Command 127

Licking Faces 129
Motivation 131
Mouthing 134
Neutering 136
Obesity 138
Old Age 140
Passive Training 142
Playing 146
Play Training 148
Pulling 153
Punishment 155
Recall 157
Retrieving 165
Reward Training 170
Roaming 173
Rolling in Muck 174
Second Home 175
Shaping 178
Showing 180
Sit 186
Socialisation 190
Speak on Command 193
Submissiveness 195
Supersense 198
Tail Chasing 202
Tail Wagging 203
Teaching Methods 206
Thieving 208
Timing 212
Toys 214
Training 217
Travelling 224
Treats 228
Tricks 230
Triggers 232
Unpredictable Behaviour 234
Unusual Behaviour 236
Urinating Indoors 239
Visitors 241
Walking to Heel 243
Working Dogs 246
Worms 249
Young Dogs 250
Conclusion 252
Index 254

Preface

This book is designed to help the dog owner understand his/her dog's behaviour, and thus have a happy relationship with a well-behaved dog. It will be of help to the person who buys a new puppy, the person whose dog develops problems along the way, as well as the person who has acquired a dog with problems.

It is laid out as an A–Z guide so that you can go directly to a section if you have a particular problem, or you can work through the alphabet, broadening your knowledge as you go.

However, I do suggest that everyone begin by reading the Introduction which explains how a dog thinks. Once you have a basic understanding of the canine mentality, dog training will be made much easier. This knowledge will help you tremendously in training your dog to be a happy, acceptable member of the community. Some of the other very important sections that you will find in the A–Z are 'Timing,' 'Motivation,' and 'Training.'

I draw my experience from many years of training my own and other people's dogs of all breeds, both as a professional and as an enthusiast. I have spent the last few years in the enviable position of being able to watch and research many different dogs' reactions to circumstances, and have used my findings to teach my pupils how to have a happy pet and a good working relationship with their dog. I hope that this book helps to give you an insight into how to enjoy your dog and not to lose your temper when things do not go according to plan. Read on.......

Acknowledgements

While writing this book, thoughts come flooding back of the people who, over the years, have contributed to the greater understanding of the subject, and to the motivation and enthusiasm that keep you striving for greater things. From the very start of my doggy career in a church hall, which housed the first bunch of enthusiastic doggy folk whom I came across, these people showed me a side to the canine world that I did not know existed. Then, as I travelled throughout the country, I encountered new ideas and thoughts on various sections of the world of dogs. The people involved are far too numerous to mention by name, but nevertheless I thank them all for their contributions.

I am very fortunate in having a family that has supported me in all aspects of my life, but in particular Michael, my husband, without whose constant encouragement, enthusiasm, and pushing this book may never have been written. The photographs were in the main taken by my husband Michael whose newly discovered talent is now much in demand in the canine world. A few of the shots were contributed by other doggy friends. Many thanks to you all.

The help of my good friend Tom Newbould in the final edit of the manuscript was invaluable. My Yorkshire accent has a tendency to spill over into my sentences sometimes, and Tom expertly and meticulously combed the text making sure that understanding the content was not restricted to those privileged to have been born in this beautiful county.

Author Angela White in her study.

Enjoy your dog, and be his partner. Encourage and guide him. Reap the rewards of a relationship that can be rivalled by no other.

‒About the Author

Angela White was born in Yorkshire, England and developed an early obsession for dogs. As a child she used to wade through old newspapers and magazines cutting out any snippets connected with dogs. She also devoted her spare time to rearing and showing cavies (guinea pigs) as a substitute to quell her craving for her own dogs. At eighteen she set up her own home, and the canine family has been steadily growing ever since.

Her working career started as an animal technician at the University of Hull, Zoology department, and she was later employed as a security-dog handler for the Ministry of Defence. As her experience with dogs grew, so did her yearning to expand her horizons. She regularly competes at Obedience shows and gained Instructors Qualifications with Honours at the British Institute of Professional Dog Trainers. She now has her own dog training centre with her husband Michael, and helps others to enjoy their dogs as much as she does her own. They also hold regular summer camps, courses and training sessions for all levels. Angela also conducts her own research on dog behaviour both at the centre and in peoples' homes where problems have occurred. She has helped with a vast variety of dog problems from chewing carpets to curing championship level competition problems; she has even trained professional security dogs and their handlers.

She is co-founder and Editor of the *Obedience Competitor Magazine*, a specialist publication on competitive dog training. She breeds and competes with her own strain of Border Collies and working sheepdogs and is regularly invited to judge at all levels.

She is also the author of *Happy Dogs‒Happy Winners: How to Keep Competition Work Enjoyable For You, Your Dog, and All Who Watch.*

What is it that makes a dog tick? Young or old, if you understand the hows and whys of canine behaviour, you can train your dog.

Introduction:

Understanding the Doggy Mind

The importance of understanding the mind of the dog cannot be emphasized sufficiently. Not understanding leads to unnecessary, ineffective, corrective methods of training that are not pleasurable to you or your dog.

Dog training should be a pleasure, not a chore or a worry. Start off on the right track, and your partnership can be rivalled by none other.

The brain of the dog works rather like a computer. Information is entered in a way that it can be understood, and it is stored. This information then can be drawn on when the correct 'buttons' or 'triggers' are pressed to recall the information. Unfortunately, unlike a computer, the dog does not always get the message first time. For example, when we show a dog what we mean by the command 'sit,' the information must be shown to the dog several times

and in exactly the same manner, each time simultaneous with the command of 'sit.' The trap which we fall into as humans is to assume the dog has got the message too soon, and so we say, 'Sit, Sit, SIT!' The dog finally sits as you start to put in some action that triggers the sit reaction; but, if you think of it, the dog is starting to learn that a human wants him to sit when he says, 'SIT, SIT, SIT, SIT!' and not on the first command of 'sit.' So we have to be very careful that through our own actions we don't inadvertently train the dog to accept bad habits that he thinks are correct. How is he to know you mean it the first time, when you always say it four times in a row? He's more astute than you think at responding to commands and signals, but not clever enough to be a mind reader.

The more kind and effective

you are as a trainer, the quicker the dog learns new things, because he gets used to the learning procedure, understands your actions, and trusts you.

The dog cannot think backwards or forwards, he can only react to *now*. If you go away and leave him in kennels, he doesn't think, 'The rotten lot fancy going off to Tenerife and leaving me in this smelly kennel with that horrible grumpy retriever as a neighbour; I'll teach them when they come home; I'll chew up so many slippers that they'll need a mortgage to replace them.'

Can you imagine if a dog could really think like that, what living with him would be like? I dread to think.

Although we might find it hard to understand with our human emotions, I'm afraid that when a dog goes into kennels he reacts to that situation only, forgetting about us until we return and give him the visual stimulus on meeting us.

A well-socialised, well-adjusted dog will make just as much, if not more, fuss of the kennel maid, each time he sees her, as he would of his owner—greeting her like a long lost friend. In some kennels the dogs are exceptionally well treated, and dogs respond accordingly when they come on a return visit. The information trigger in their brain connects kennels with either a pleasant experience, 'let me in,' or a bad experience, 'let me out.' It is not necessarily the fault of the kennels, as it can be caused by the owners' failing to socialise the dog properly, and so the dog is frightened of new experiences.

Therefore, the more good experiences that your dog is able to gather, the more he is able to react in a desirable manner to new ones, because his brain connection then says, 'New experience, let's investigate, it should be fun.'

Too many bad experiences and the dog finds it difficult to approach anything new with optimism. He becomes what I suppose in human terms would be classed as an introvert. Also, because he is after all an animal, if the situation feels too intense, he has only two natural impulses to follow, namely fight or flight. We then have an aggressive or a timid animal all because time was not taken by the owners to teach him that new experiences are on the whole pleasurable.

Dogs are not naturally naughty. The only things bad about dogs are the people who train them. You can guarantee that, if a dog is misbehaving, it's because he doesn't understand that what he's doing at that moment is wrong in the eyes of us humans.

By far the best method of training is to show the dog correctly, patiently, and repeatedly what is wanted, giving praise for that action whilst he is doing it. Only when you are absolutely sure that the dog understands that the command you give is to trigger the action you require should you try the command without all of the help the dog needed to get him there.

If the dog is doing something wrong, he must be caught in the very act and shown what is right. It's no use catching him half an hour later and telling him off for fouling on the carpet. Yes, he understands you are cross, but he cannot think why. All he thinks of is

what is happening there and then, which is probably coming to say, 'Hello,' as you come through the door. He doesn't know what's wrong. If you catch him even a few seconds after, he cannot connect your anger with what he did wrong. All he knows is that you are annoyed—but with what he has no idea. His reaction is likely to sculk off out of the way, which leads you to think to yourself that he knows he's done wrong. I'm sorry to disappoint you, but he does not.

Correction must be done *simultaneously* with the act. No amount of chastising will make any difference after the event, not even one second after. He just will not understand. Even if it makes you feel better to scold him after you find a mess, just think of it from his point of view: every time he comes to greet you he gets aggression, be it physical or verbal, and it is not a pleasurable experience. What is he to think when he's loose in the park and you're calling him? It is a much more pleasurable experience to carry on having a sniff and a romp, is it not?

In actual fact, correction is

not really the best method of training. It is far better to prevent the dog from making mistakes where possible, always showing him the right way at the start, just as we do with children.

Inevitably dogs sometimes do things that, although may be quite normal to them, are unacceptable to us. In these instances, the best policy is to ignore those things. Do something to distract him and show him the right way to carry on, always making it interesting to do the right things and most uninteresting to do the wrong ones.

The moral is get it right the first time. Be clear and precise in your actions. If the dog is going wrong, think 'Why?'—not 'Wallop.' He is only reacting to the stimuli around him.

The author's beloved and well-trained Oscar. Photo by J. Midgley.

Adolescence

Dogs go through adolescence at varying ages. In general, the larger the breed, the later adolescence occurs. The character and upbringing of your dog has a distinct bearing on how this stage shows itself. We are, of course, talking of the stage, as in humans, when the young pup starts to realise that he is growing into a 'proper' dog. It can be a most frustrating time for the owners, if the young dog has not had a well-controlled upbringing, and it is at this stage that most people shout, 'Help!'

Adolescent dogs are often likened to juvenile delinquents, and they really need to be treated in a similar way—with a firm but loving hand guiding them into the correct,

Young dogs will react to the situation in front of them. Teach them the correct way to react because, like children, they will go the unacceptable way if not guided correctly.

acceptable pattern of behaviour.

Many pups who have been

treated rather like a spoilt toddler and allowed to choose what they want to do all the time—eat on demand, play on demand, and be exercised on demand—now start to turn into, in their own eyes, pack leaders who must always get their own way. Many people are even more lenient with their dog than they ever would dream of being with a child, and the calls for help come loudly and fast, as the dog starts to realise that he has you at his beck and call.

If you have your dog from a pup, set the correct ground rules for your pet and stick by them. Remember to be fair. Don't expect the dog to cope with rules to which he is not capable of adhering. Like a well-reared child who knows that, if bedtime is 8:00 pm, then 8:00 pm is when it is, and will conform with a minimum of fuss, so too will a well-raised dog heed your command and obey your rules. Set your rules and stick by them.

Often the adolescent stage is the time when your dog starts to 'go deaf.' As new smells come his way, he seems to ignore your calls and commands in the park. These problems can be avoided if you follow the guidelines set down in each relevant section. For example, if your dog suddenly starts to ignore you when you want him back, turn to the section on recall. Better still, if your dog is still young and you have not encountered any problems yet, read through all of this book and prevent problems from happening in the first place.

Facing page, bottom: Even small breeds can become a problem if not educated correctly.

When faced with a problem, the handler's natural reaction is to become tense and hold the lead as tightly as possible—immediately transferring a message to the dog that says, 'Yes, you're right; there is something to worry about.'

Aggression

There are very few truly aggressive dogs. A truly aggressive dog would cause severe injury if he were to bite because he would direct all of his energies to it. Dogs who display this behavior seldom get the chance to do it twice, as they are normally destroyed in accordance with the law.

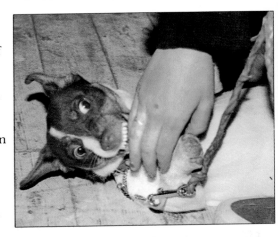

Aggression that occurs for a reason that we humans can

Relax with your dog, and he too will relax.

understand is more readily controlled or re-directed. Once the reason for the aggression has been determined, then we are on the way to the solution.

TOWARDS PEOPLE OR OTHER DOGS

Sometimes dogs bite others because they are playful. Biting is natural play behaviour for a dog. If no one makes him understand that biting is not socially acceptable in the human world, then he will carry on. But *aggression* towards others often has its roots set in fear. Although the dog may not appear to be frightened, fear is often the reason for his aggression towards strangers in particular. More often than not, the owners, albeit inadvertently, have taught the dog to be aggressive towards strangers.

Fear biting often starts with the dog's barking or simply backing off because he is wary of strangers, which is a natural canine reaction. When owners try to rectify the situation by pushing the dog forward, the dog cannot run away, and so he bites. This escalation of behaviour often happens so quickly as we reinforce the dog's reactions, that we are unable to think back to the start, and cannot believe that we are in any way to blame for our dog's biting, when it's the very thing we were trying to prevent. This problem and its solution are explained in the chapter on fearfulness.

Many dog owners, when approached by a stranger, react

by shortening and tightening the lead, tensing up and holding on as tightly as possible. The dog feels this action, becomes convinced that there must be something to worry about, and so becomes on his guard. The handler doesn't need to react like that more than once with a dog who is already unsure of himself to create a problem that takes some curing. If you are not careful, the problem can be heightened by your attempts to eradicate it.

When a dog comes to our training school and reacts timidly or fearfully towards strangers, we teach the handler to take away the tension of the situation by getting up and walking away from the problem. We also teach the owner how to play with his dog (see Playing), so that instead of getting tension and fear from the handler as a stranger approaches the dog gets fun and pleasure and a relaxed atmosphere. After a little work, the dog comes to associate the approach of a stranger with something pleasurable and not apprehensive.

It may come as a shock to you that, in the author's opinion, you shouldn't scold a dog for showing aggression to others. It will certainly seem

The instinct to guard is very strong in some breeds, and this drive must be properly directed.

odd to the strangers who approach if they do not understand dogs, but you must remember that aggression fought with aggression only breeds more aggression.

It is important that you not

put people at risk, so, until you have perfected your timing and playing and sharpened your reactions and awareness of situations, do not let people get too close but rather simply walk away and distract your dog so as not to heighten the situation, nor risk the chance of a bite.

TOWARDS FAMILY MEMBERS

This type of aggression has its roots in the dominance role. If the dog shows any form of aggression in any situation, particularly in the house, then the dog possesses some degree of dominance over you or the person at whom the aggression is directed. Even though you may not agree, in the dog's eyes he has the edge. How to recognise dominance and dominant aggression and how to deal with it is covered in the section on dominance.

OVER FOOD

This is one of the most common forms of aggression. It is normal for a dog to protect his food: it is the type of behaviour that all dogs would learn in order to survive in the wild. But, we do not live in the

wild, and it is not necessary to protect your food in order to survive when you are lucky enough to live in a house with humans. So the dog must learn from the start, if possible, that it's just not done!

We can inadvertently encourage our dogs to be protective over food by making it easy for them to defend it— for instance, if we put their dish in a quiet corner and/or leave them in peace to eat. So by what might be termed passive training (see Passive Training), the dog learns that no one comes near his food. When he is a puppy and growls as you come close to his bowl, you are inclined to think of it as cute or showing that he's growing up. But, left to develop, it can become a serious problem. It is not sufficient to tell everyone to keep away whilst he's eating although it might be good advice to prevent an accident, because sometime or another someone will make the mistake of getting too close, and you never quite trust a dog again once he has bitten, especially if he bites a child.

When conditioning a young pup, stay with him whilst he is

eating; touch him, handle his dish and food, and teach him that there is no need to protect his nourishment. If you already have this problem with your adult dog, then a reconditioning programme must be followed. Whilst the training is in progress, keep other people away from his dish in order to be safe.

To start the reconditioning process, change your dog's feeding place. If it was in a corner, bring it out into the open. Start off by preparing his food in a container and offering a small amount at a time by hand. Pet him, stroke him, and reassure him that his actions are good

Feed your dog piece by piece until he comes to understand that a human near his food means there is more to come—and not that his meal is threatened.

whilst he is eating. The next day prepare the food in the same manner and offer most by hand. During the feeding process, put a couple of pieces of food into his bowl, one at a time, and hold out the bowl whilst he takes the food. Do not at this stage put the bowl on the floor. Continue the meal by feeding from your hand, petting him all the while. The next day you can offer a small amount of food on the dish, still holding it in your hand, and then replenish it with a little more, so that the dog becomes accustomed to the dish's being taken away, and then receiving more food. No longer does a hand near his bowl mean that he is going to lose his food. Don't forget to keep reassuring him, and take it step by step. Once he will accept your placing food in his bowl and replenishing it whilst the bowl is still in your hand, you can re-start the procedure, one morsel at a time, putting the bowl down on the floor, and lifting it each time to replenish it. It is a good idea to start this crucial stage by having some really tasty morsels to replenish the bowl. If you are in the least bit worried, have the dog on a lead so that you can guide him away from his bowl. If he shows any sign of aggression start at the beginning again and take the steps more slowly. If the training is taken gradually and carefully, the dog will soon learn that there is plenty of food to go 'round, and thus it is not necessary to guard his bowl. He will learn that by eagerly standing away from his bowl he stands a good chance of receiving an extra tasty titbit.

When you are absolutely certain that there is no aggression, you can start at step one again, but this time with another member of the family feeding him (not a small child at this stage). By repeating this procedure with different people, you teach the dog that everyone is a friend and that no one is a threat to his food.

Appetite

Dogs' appetites change for a variety of reasons. Quite often there is a simple explanation. As puppies grow older, their need for food gradually increases, and then decreases when they approach adulthood. Many pups as they develop will not want one of their meals, and it is quite normal for them to walk away from the food that you so lovingly prepared. Pups normally start to reject or be disinterested in one of their meals between four and six months of age. The pup himself is your best guide as long as he maintains a reasonable weight, continues to grow, and doesn't refuse all food.

Elderly dogs typically need less food as their metabolisms and exercise levels decrease. They sometimes benefit from being fed small, more frequent meals, like those fed to puppies.

The most likely reason for a ferocious appetite, coupled with a very lean body, is worms. All dogs should be regularly checked for the presence of worms by a veterinarian.

Dogs under stress, such as those in temporary kennels or experiencing a change of home, may lose their appetite for a while; but, no harm usually comes of this, and they are pretty soon back to normal. Any sudden change in appetite, or even a gradual change, should be reported to your vet. Take your pet in for a checkup to be on the safe side.

There are various appetite boosters available. I have always found natural herbal additives the best. Kelp can help to improve appetite in my experience, as does a regular exercise programme, coupled with plenty of constructive training, playing, a stable home environment, and adequate rest.

Barking

Barking is a fundamental means of canine communication. It is a basic part of dog ownership.

To many owners, consistent barking is one of the most aggravating noises to bear. We must realize, however, that barking is one of the dog's basic means of communication. Birds sing, cats meow, children chatter, dogs bark!

It would be very cruel to insist that a dog never bark, and often there are times when we might want him to, such as when an intruder is around.

Starting from scratch, it's much better to encourage your dog to bark by giving a command. Each time Oscar barks and I'm near him, I say, 'Good boy, speak.' I take him into situations where I know he'll want to bark. I stand by his side, my hand holding his collar, and whisper, "What's that?" in an excited, secretive tone. When he starts to look around, expecting something to happen, and I can feel the tension and hear the low grumble starting, I say, 'Good boy Oscar, speak,' and the grumble accelerates into a bark. And so step by step he starts to learn to bark as I say, 'Speak.' All the while he is confidently barking, I carry on encouraging him. I watch carefully, and, as any signs of his stopping appear, I turn him away from the situation and say, 'Good boy Oscar, quiet.' And so he is quiet—partly because he wants to be, but also because I said so.

With encouragement for barking and praise for stopping, the dog learns to bark at your command. Each time he barks of his own accord, I go up to him immediately and say, 'Good boy Oscar, speak.' I encourage him for a few moments, then turn him away from whatever he is barking at and say, 'Good boy, quiet.' Eventually he will stop barking immediately, and I say, 'Good boy, quiet.' He is never scolded for doing what comes naturally, only praised and controlled.

It is a wonderful thing to know that, if you are approached by an intruder or attacker, your dog will bark on command. It doesn't mean that he is aggressive, and he is under your control the whole time, but most intruders will go elsewhere when they see your control over your dog. Most dogs taught like this will only bother to bark when there is reason, e.g., an intruder or

stranger comes around your property.

If you live in a highly populated area and your dog can see people passing by all the time, take him out to experience the people going by on a very regular basis so that he can see that there is nothing to be worried about by this regular occurrence. He soon will learn to react only if someone actually comes to your door.

Many people give a dog a titbit or biscuit to 'shut him up.' If you think a little more into it, what you are training your dog to do is bark for food or reward. Whenever the dog is well behaved or quiet, he is more or less ignored. As soon as he is 'naughty,' he is rewarded with a titbit or by your going to him and holding him while he barks. Think of it logically: there is no reward for being quiet, so he must naturally think that to get your attention he must bark. So plan your training programme, organise yourself so that you can pay more attention to your dog, and take him into situations where you can tell him to bark.

BARKING IN YOUR ABSENCE

Most dogs bark when left on their own because they are confined to one room, the yard, or a kennel, and they react to this isolation by barking. The same dog, given the run of the house or garden, may well be quiet. This freedom may not be possible because of the dog's destructiveness or soiling in the house, but these are problems that can be eradicated with proper training.

Other dogs react to specific situations, e.g., they bark only at specific things such as traffic or other dogs that can be seen or heard from the house.

Try to determine why the dog actually barks (it may be for more than one reason). Rather than scolding the dog, take him away from those bark stimuli. For instance, if the dog barks at an unanswered telephone or doorbell, these can be disconnected. If he barks at outside noises, a radio can help to mask all but the loudest noises. If he is disturbed by passing children at the front of the house, confine him to the back area.

The most important thing to remember is that, if you are not there, you cannot stop him, so take away from his hearing the things that make him bark excessively. Your dog's hearing is many times more sensitive than your own, so consider very carefully and try to work out all those things that make him react. Once you have masked or eliminated all of the stimuli, you can confidently leave him. However, still set up a training programme that teaches him to bark only when told, as described in the opening of this section.

If your dog barks for no other reason than your absence, set up a situation having eliminated as many bark stimuli as possible. Leave quietly. Go back in and praise him. If he starts barking, burst in at full steam while banging an old pan with a metal object as hard as you can. The sudden noise is unpleasant, of course. Go out again. If he remains quiet for a few moments, return quietly and praise him. Repeat this many times. Some dogs will learn to wait until your footsteps have gone, so imitate the sound of your walking away, and then keep quiet, or walk away a few steps and then tiptoe back. At the first bark, burst in making as much noise as possible; then go out again. Wait a few moments. If he is quiet, go in quietly and praise him gently.

If you set aside time to do this training session and can concentrate and follow it through without actually going away from the house at all, you may well be able to cure it in one session. Timing is all important in this and all other dog training. Make sure that you are bursting in only when he barks, and going in gently to praise him only when he is quiet.

If your dog barks at people, dogs, traffic, etc., whilst you are out walking, don't go back into your shell and say, "I can't take him out because he barks at things or people." This sort of barking occurs because he is frightened or doesn't understand. Take him out as much as you can. Introduce him to things from a distance,

If your dog barks at other dogs or people, then training classes are an excellent place to help him overcome any anxieties that he may have.

assuring him that things are OK.

If he barks at traffic, take him into the middle of a car park and walk around the stationary cars to let him have a good look. Take him gently up to a car with its engine running, reassuring him all the time. Take things step by step and let him learn that those great big metal 'animals' are not going to get him, so he doesn't need to bark to frighten them off.

If he barks at other dogs or people, then get amongst them more. Join a dog club where people understand your problems. Socialise, you'll probably find people in the dog club with far worse problems than yours, and also people with lots of patience to say, 'Hello,' and offer your dog a titbit and the hand of friendship. You'll find dogs with good temperament who just want to say, 'Hello,' and your dog will learn rapidly that life is fun.

Remember that all training must be done on lead so that you have complete control. It is also essential that your dog be adequately exercised and mentally stimulated. Many owners of small dogs seem to be under the impression that their dogs don't need much exercise, but this is quite untrue. All dogs need exercise—some more than others agreed—but more importantly all dogs need mental stimulation.

Additionally, by taking him for walks along the busy streets, he learns to accept all of those things that might otherwise make him bark, as they cease to become a big deal.

A training programme with your dog that teaches him all the basic commands, e.g., sit, down, stand, fetch, will stimulate his brain. A good training session is more tiring for a dog than a stroll 'round the block. A tired dog will settle down and sleep for the best part of the time that you are absent, as long as his basic needs have been satisfied. A dog deprived of his basic needs becomes frustrated, which leads to barking, chewing, and other undesirable behaviors.

If your dog is very noisy or barks at night, it is a good idea to take him out to a place where no one minds and encourage him to have a good bark. No dog barks for 24 hours a day. So, if you give the dog opportunity to really have a good bark, you stand more chance of the quiet moments fitting into your domestic arrangements.

Bedtime

As with all other aspects of your dog's life, enforcing the bedtime rules requires that the dog know where he stands (or rather lies down!).

To establish a setting conducive to training, choose a safe comfortable place, an easily accessible place, one preferably containing his own bed or at least his own blanket, and teach him gently but firmly the word 'bed' in connection with the place where you want him to sleep.

Armed with some titbits, and your dog on lead, take him to the bed and encourage him to get in it, gently laying him down in the bed, giving him the titbits. Keep repeating the command 'bed' and give lots of praise. Guide him out of the bed, still on the lead, and repeat the procedure. Lay him down in the bed saying, 'Oscar, bed, good boy.' Give him the titbit and then lead him out again. Repeat this exercise a few times at each training session.

In the bed he receives affection and a titbit. He must not associate the word 'bed' with a punishment or bad experience. Repeat this training session several times each day until your dog learns that the bed is a good safe place to go where he will not be disturbed. He can then be sent there at any time of day, and will understand that he should stay there until told otherwise.

When it is really bedtime, make sure that your dog has been well fed and exercised and has been allowed to relieve himself. I always go out with Oscar just before bedtime and give him his command to eliminate (see Housetraining). I then take him to the place where he is to sleep, give him a biscuit or chew and water, and leave him to it.

It is important that you make a sensible decision about where your dog should sleep and stick to it. If at the first sign of a whimper, you go rushing in and cuddle him and let him come and sleep with you after deciding that the kitchen or out-house was to be his bedroom, then he will quickly learn that to make a noise will result in his getting what he wants, at which point problems start to emerge.

If you wish to have your dog in the bedroom with you, it is fine, but it should be your decision and not

which I did by getting out of bed and showing him what I wanted, calmly, quietly, and without harsh words.

Dogs like to have a place to call their own. Just make sure that the place selected is mutually agreeable and not determined solely by the dog.

his. Oscar has his own bed in my bedroom and knows that 'bed' means 'stay there until morning,' and he does. He is not allowed to climb onto my bed. Of course, he tried once or twice, but I always insisted that he get off and return to his bed,

Do not be tempted to yell commands from your bed, as this will enforce the fact in the dog's mind that he does not necessarily have to obey every time. Get up and show him what you want. You will get more sleep in the long run!

Biting

If the dog is biting you or other people in a vicious fashion, it usually is an extension of aggression in most cases, and you would be wise to read the section on aggression. Sometimes dogs will bite their own bodies, which is usually a sign that something is amiss medically or psychologically. A call to the vet is the most sensible route. Often a dog will continue biting himself even after an illness has cleared, because it becomes force of habit.

The dog's biting himself is easy to stop if you are always with him. Simply stop him physically yet gently and give the command 'No.' Distract him, and praise him as soon as he has stopped. But as we cannot all have eyes in the back of our head, we can buy a

This dog is playing with the lead, biting and pulling. Use a favourite toy or titbit to distract him from the lead. Don't pull against him or he will think you are joining in the game.

If biting is a compulsive behaviour brought about by boredom, then plenty of exercise may be the simple cure.

type of collar usually called a bucket (as this is what people used to use) or Elizabethan collar that fits around the neck and prevents the dog from reaching around to bite himself. This device soon breaks the habit if that is all it was. Dogs sometimes bite themselves through boredom, which can be an indication that life needs to be a bit more interesting and the environment more stimulating (see Compulsive Behaviour, Unusual Behaviour).

A lot of dogs have a tendency to grab your hand with their mouth, which is not really vicious biting though still quite painful sometimes. It can become more serious if allowed to carry on, and these dogs need to be taught about bite inhibition (see Mouthing).

If your dog bites other people, read the sections on aggression and equipment; if he bites you, then the sections on aggression and more importantly dominance are the ones you should turn to straightaway.

LEAD BITING

Sometimes, when walking to heel, the dog will keep biting or holding the lead in his mouth and pulling. This behaviour is normally the result of excitement and the desire to have a game; but, sometimes the dog holds on to the lead to prevent you from pulling it. If you have been using the lead as a play toy to gain his attention, simply use a toy to distract him from the lead and divert his attention to something less troublesome. Alternatively you can just refuse to pull against the lead, thus taking away the enjoyment of the game. In my opinion the best thing to do, if you find it troublesome, is to divert the game to a toy or rope tug-tease. This way you're not distressing the dog in any way and he will not be put off. (see also Play Training.)

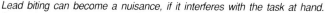

Lead biting can become a nuisance, if it interferes with the task at hand.

Breeding

Before deciding to breed, you must first consider many things. The most important points I will now discuss:

1. If your bitch successfully produces a litter of healthy bouncing puppies, are you sure that you will have sufficient caring homes for them? If someone changes his mind or wants to go on holiday first, are you in a position to keep those puppies longer than originally anticipated? Bear in mind that it is not unusual for large breeds like German Shepherd Dogs to have ten puppies.

2. Are you financially in a position to pay a stud fee? Pay for the veterinary care, especially if something goes wrong? Will you be able to stand the loss of all of the puppies if things go very wrong, bearing in mind that the vet and probably the stud dog owner will still want to be paid? Can you afford the extra food for the bitch whilst she is pregnant and lactating, and then for the puppies whose appetites will get larger?

3. Puppies in a whelping box are fine for the first two to three weeks, but after that you will have puppies everywhere if you don't arrange a separate area where they can be confined. Puppies need to be able to get out of the whelping box and defecate; and, if you do not clean up quickly enough, they will roll in what they have just deposited—and so will their fellow pups!

4. Are you mentally hard enough to take pups with physical defects to the vet to be euthanised?

5. Are you prepared to stay up all night while your bitch produces the little bundles? Do you know enough to help her if she gets into difficulties?

6. Are you prepared to act as foster mum and feed pups every two hours if your bitch cannot?

7. If, after you have sold your pups, someone decides that he can't cope for whatever reason, are you prepared to take the dog back until a new home can be found?

It is best to leave breeding to the experts. Puppies are extremely trying and a great responsibility, even after you have sent them to their new homes.

8. What will you do if the German Shepherd Dog whom you sold for working collapses with the hereditary disease of hip displasia, or the Collie whom you sold to the farmer has PRA (another hereditary disease) and goes blind? Many pedigreed dogs have some form of hereditary disease or defect common to them. Do you know those peculiar to your breed? Do you know how to recognise the signs and how to get the dog tested before mating?

9. Can you cope if your bitch or dog passes a genetic defect that no one knew was there and the whole litter is affected by it? Defects like haemophilia and hermaphrodites occur sometimes, and even the most experienced breeders are helpless to the seemingly uncontrollable side of genetics.

10. Does your bitch really possess qualities that are to the good of the breed and worth passing on to future generations? Will the qualities of your chosen stud dog make a good match genetically?

Well, have I deterred you yet? If not, then you are made of stern stuff and will probably make a good breeder, providing you know enough about genetics, anatomy, reproduction and nutrition— that is without touching on the subject of how to achieve a successful mating in the first place, which is not always as easy as it sounds.

Choosing and purchasing a puppy is a big step for most people, and it is the responsibility of the breeder to both the pup and the prospective owner to take all possible steps to ensure that the partnership is the right one. As the breeder you need to have the strength of character to turn away people who are not suitable (by their circumstances or temperament) to own your particular breed.

Not everyone would get on with Oscar: he's lively, bouncy, hairy, and forever in the mud,

but *we* love him and make provisions for him. We acquired Oscar from a rescue centre at nine months old. His previous owners could not cope—they didn't realise what a handful he would be. They had probably seen dogs like Oscar standing quietly in the show ring, but had not been told of all the training, hard work, and understanding that goes into controlling this permanently coiled spring eager to be released.

Breeders must inform people of all the drawbacks specific to the breed, as well as the good points, and explain fully what the pup's behaviour could be like as it starts to mature.

Many people come to me and say that they bought a retriever or collie because they had seen them working on TV and they always look so well behaved. Surely the breeders should have told them of the hours and hours of expert training that go into making a sheepdog look so controlled, or a guide dog take a blind person for a stroll. It is not automatic, and breeders have a moral obligation to tell people. If the prospective purchasers are still keen, knowing all the pitfalls, then, great.

Breeders must be able to advise the new owners on nutrition, training classes, and the general well-being of the dog, and have an open door to any problems that the new owners may have for the good of the animal, and his life with his new family.

If you still want to breed, then go for it! You are just what dogs need—a caring, responsible breeder who breeds to the good of the animal and not just for financial gain. If, on the other hand, you are put off by any of my points, then breeding is not for you. It is not an obligation to enter the complicated world of breeding just because you choose to own a dog. If you don't, the ever capacity-filled rescue centres will thank you for being so sensible.

Proper breeding is not child's play. It is best left to the experts. Photo of happy youngster and Newfoundland pups by R. Reagan.

Cages/Crates ———

Quite often dogs are kept for short periods of time in large metal crates, either for their own protection against bigger or aggressive dogs or for the protection of the owner's car or home. Cages are great if used sensibly: as long as the dog is well exercised and not left caged for too long, crates can solve all sorts of problems. Destructiveness is one of the main reasons for caging young adults or pups. Confined to his own space, the dog does not have the opportunity to chew your best Chippendale or Wilton! Fouling is also controlled, as a dog has to be pretty desperate to foul the place where he has to sleep. For young pups and excitable dogs, crates also make travelling safer.

Once acclimated to the cage, most dogs happily enter and treat it as a place of refuge. Many will go in of their own accord if the gate is left open in the house. But, remember, if you want to cage your dog, be sure that he has plenty of freedom, too. It would be most unfair to leave him caged for very long periods of time or in direct sunlight—use your common sense and be fair to your dog. Cages are great for families who do not have facilities to put their dogs outside in the garden for a break. Sometimes it's easier to get on with chores if the dog is not under your feet, and it's better for the dog if he's not continually chastised by a busy pre-occupied human.

When choosing a cage, pick one that will be big enough for your dog to lie down flat, and one that will be strong enough to hold him. Make sure there are no sharp edges, and that the gate has a good fixing. Collapsible cages are ideal as they fold down flat when not in use. I am a great believer in cages used for the right reasons, but I always take care to make sure that the dog's needs are satisfied. One other point, with smaller breeds and puppies make sure that the bars are close enough together so that the dog cannot get his head, legs, or mouth stuck. There is nothing more chilling to the spine than the sound of a puppy with his mouth or head stuck between the bars, as I know from my own experience (we all have to learn somehow). I hope that my experiences will help you not to make the same mistakes!

Collapsible cages are great because they fold up for easy storage and transport. Photo by I. Français of Soft Coated Wheaten Terrier owned by L. Lockquell.

Chasing

Does your dog chase people, traffic, other dogs, or livestock? If so then you must consider why. Does he want to play? Is he frightened? Is he expressing dominance or aggression? Look very carefully, as the differences between fear and aggression/dominance are sometimes difficult to recognise. A fearful dog may chase; but, if the object or animal comes towards him, he will turn and run. He chases in the first place on the basis of getting in the first bite, so to speak. He tries to say, 'I'm the boss,' in the hope that whatever it is that he is chasing will say, 'OK,' and go away! A truly dominant dog chases to say, 'I AM the boss, clear off, go away from my territory or else!' (See also Aggression, Dominance, Fearfulness.)

Most dogs, however, chase because they are happy-go-lucky and want to have a game or simply say, 'Hello.' This behaviour can unfortunately be rather disconcerting to strangers. With stories every week in the media telling how children or adults have been savagely attacked by uncontrolled dogs, who can blame people for being afraid when even the friendliest of dogs comes bounding up with the owner, either yelling at the top of his voice, obviously having lost control and trying to get it back, or entirely ignoring the dog and pretending that he doesn't belong to him? For you as an owner, there's nothing more embarrassing than that helpless feeling you have when you lose control of your dog.

And so to the plan of action for solving this distressing problem. Unless you are a pretty fast sprinter (which I'm not!), there is little point in joining the chase, because it is exactly how the dog will see it— 'Oh good, dad is joining in, too.' There are some basic exercises, however, that will help you.

Control can be taught at a distance with a long lead—teaching your dog that it is always more pleasurable to be with you than to go his own way.

They are the down (instant) and the come (recall). Also consider reward and distraction training. Turn to the appropriate sections for the methods to teach them.

Even when the dog understands the commands 'come' and 'down', what you may find is that the dog will seemingly go deaf as soon as he sees something to chase—he will forget all about you, and leave you yelling at the top of your voice again. To prevent this from happening, take things step by step. As usual complete control can be maintained only if you have your dog on the lead. I would suggest that you now use a longer lead (one of the good quality extending leads are ideal because they retract back into the handle, taking in the slack). But if your budget doesn't stretch that far, a length of garden clothes line or strong rope provides a reasonable alternative. Take your dog to a situation where he is likely to give chase to something, give him some slack on the lead, and relax and let him do as he pleases. As soon as there's a chance that he has seen something to chase, but before he has chance to react, call his name with the command 'come,' and reel him in. As he comes back to you, give him lots of praise. Remember that you are always Mr. Nice Guy. You will find it useful to couple the praise with the production of a favourite toy (see Play Training).

Some people try this method and report that, as soon as they take the lead off, the dog ignores their commands again. If this happens then you haven't given it enough time. It may take quite a few weeks of consistent training for the dog to understand that you mean what you say every time, and not just sometimes. The very act of the chase has given the dog great pleasure, and has been sufficient reward to make him want to do it again. Remember that whatever he wants to chase must be interesting, so you must make it your business to be even more interesting than that distraction.

When out walking with Oscar, I always look around me frequently to make sure that there are no loose dogs or children around to tempt him. Oscar loves children and finds it difficult to control his urge to rush over and cover them in kisses. So I always call him to me and put him on lead before he sees them, and then we can go over to say 'Hello' without the children being frightened to death by this great hairy lump bounding towards them.

So think ahead, think of others, and think for your dog. Take all precautions possible to avoid the chase in the first place. If your dog does take flight unexpectedly, use your instant down command to drop him in his tracks. Dogs respond to this instant authority much more than they do to the recall. I practice the instant down frequently while I'm out and Oscar is loose so that it becomes a natural part of the game; and, in the event of an emergency, I can drop him, and then just walk over and attach his lead.

Chewing

To prevent your dog from chewing your furniture, provide him with something that is interesting to chew—and safe.

The first question that we must ask is 'Why do dogs chew?'

Before you can set about stopping a dog from chewing your belongings and furniture, it is important to understand why he chews in the first place.

In the wild, a dog's survival depends on his having healthy teeth and gums. Without these vital tools, killing and eating one's lunch becomes pretty difficult. In the absence of toothpaste and brush, dogs opt for chewing on wood, old bones, hooves, or hide from previous kills to help clean and care for their teeth. It is their instinct to chew to clean away debris from their teeth. Chewing means survival.

In modern society the dog is chews the furniture. Well, imagine yourself in the dog's place, particularly when he is left to his own devices. No need to search for food, the dog has much free time. The natural thing to do when nothing else demands your attention is to look after your physique: a

The Tug-A-Bone is a proven safe tug toy that will provide many hours of healthy fun.*

often given many chew toys, and frustrated owners cannot work out why the dog still

quick wash and brush up and then to the matter of oral hygiene. As the dog looks around for a likely chew, he sees many suitable (in his eyes) objects—a lump of wood (your antique gate-leg table), a piece of hide (your best leather shoes), and so on. Of course, there are the chew toys that you gave him, but how is he to know that you would rather he chew them than your furniture?

You may say, 'He doesn't do it while I'm there because he knows that he is not allowed: I caught him and told him off." But does he really understand? Dogs are not naughty or malicious; these emotions or traits are human ones. Dogs are often confused, but they try their hardest to please us. When chastised for chewing the furniture, if the timing perfect, the dog may well understand that he must not chew that item in your

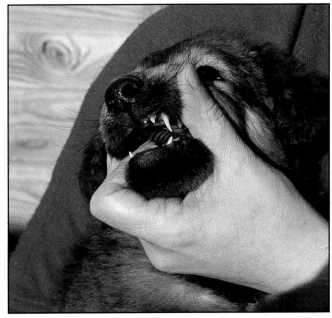

Chewing is a natural part of a puppy's teething process, and it must be directed to appropriate outlets—not one's fingers. Photo by S. Miller.

presence. But why should he connect it to mean the same in your absence? He may well have chewed in your absence in the past and nothing hostile happened—in fact he derived great pleasure from it. So he assumes that it must be OK. And who can blame him? He has absolutely no reason to think otherwise.

So how do we get around the dilemma? Going back to a dog's natural make up, he tends to be more active, if left to his own devices, in the early morning and late evening (dawn and dusk). So, if a dog is left in the house for a day (too long in my opinion anyway, but say he is), he is more likely to chew just after you leave him, and then again later, towards the end of the day. So when preparing to leave him, first make sure that you have picked up all of your footwear and prized possessions; and, if at all possible, put the dog in an area where the least damage can be done, at least until we have programmed the dog into only chewing his own chews. A good selection of chew toys (check that they are safe) is a good investment. Whilst it may be a little costly it's cheaper than re-upholstering the suite! These toys and chews should be put down for the dog just before you leave, so that they are fresh and interesting. The best trick that I have found is to get a large bone from the butcher and boil it so that all the meat and juices are removed (use the water on the dog's food later).

Then take a succulent piece of cooked chicken or beef and poke it down inside the bone. The dog should be allowed to see you do this. Now the bone is the most desirable chew toy around and the dog will spend literally hours trying to get to the meat in the middle, and will probably fall asleep doing so. Chair legs and carpets suddenly look very boring. Each day, before leaving the dog, you can put into the bone a fresh flavour to keep up the novelty. When you return home at the end of the day, tell your dog to fetch his bone before you greet him; make a fuss of the bone and then put it away until tomorrow.

By doing this you are starting to make the dog associate the end of the day, your return, and his bone, thus creating an idea that starts to click into place: as the day draws to a close and his natural tendency to be more active rears its head, he sees the bone, picks it up in anticipation of the next pleasure, which is your coming home and greeting him. You are conditioning his behaviour to be desirable, whilst still

Dogs love to chew, and their chew toys often become prized objects—objects that can be used as rewards for tasks well accomplished.

allowing him his natural canine behaviour. If your dog has to be left for long periods on a regular basis, it is advisable that you arrange a kennel and run for him so that he can answer the call of nature, etc., and also the Chippendale and Wilton will not be at risk. After all, even the juiciest of bones can get boring after a while, and he will seek his environmental enrichment elsewhere (see also Cages/ Crates, Kennels). You may also find it interesting to read the section on barking. Although you may not have this specific problem, teaching your dog to accept being left in a room on his own without doing things that are undesirable to you would also benefit and help you and your dog deal with this problem.

Children and Dogs

Children and dogs can make ideal companions, provided that both learn the basics of man-and-dog interaction.

Children and dogs are alike in some ways, and, in general, those adults who have had more to do with the bringing up or coping with young children make the best or most successful dog trainers. I am sure that there are exceptions to every rule, but on the whole this is so. Children should be taught the ground rules at the very beginning when you acquire a dog so that dog, child, and the rest of the family can learn to live in harmony. Young children should never be left alone with dogs, no matter how placid the dog might be.

It must always be remembered that the dog is an animal, and also that children can be very cruel even if it is through their lack of knowledge as opposed to any malice. Research shows that young families are the most likely section of the community to have dogs. When children reach the age of eight or so, they become more aware of animals

Children should be educated as soon as possible on how to act in the presence of a dog.

as fun and often begin to pester parents about having a dog.

My young son saw a documentary programme on the television, showing the destruction of abandoned and unwanted dogs. He immediately wanted to go out and save them, particularly the rather cute and cuddly puppy whose appealing eyes left a pang of pity in the most hardened of people. At eight years old, he was set to save the canine world and bring them all home, if only his cruel mother would have said, 'Yes!' It's easy to be swayed into taking on a dog when maybe the time is not quite right. For the sake of the animal, do not be persuaded by the whims of your children, whose whim next week could well be a pony, a kitten, or even just the latest craze in tee-shirts.

Classes and Clubs

Dogs, like people, differ tremendously in character and temperament, but the basic methods of dog training work for most handlers. Most instructors at dog training classes start off as an enthusiastic beginner; and, as they expand their knowledge, other people start to respect their advice and opinion. Some people make excellent instructors but never excel at handling dogs, while many excellent dog handlers cannot tell you how they did it to save their lives. Some people, of course, excel in both fields, and all are worth listening to.

I started off as I describe above, an enthusiastic beginner, with my mongrel puppy from the rescue society. I learnt quickly, and things came quite naturally to me and my little pup. I will be forever grateful to my instructors for their enthusiastic welcome into the world of dog obedience.

Obedience classes are the best place to start with your dog to learn the basic art of control. Your vet should be able to tell you of the nearest group. Classes will vary with the standard of professionalism of the instructors. Many instructors are well-meaning pet owners who give up their spare time because they enjoy helping others to become responsible dog owners. Some are more enthusiastic competition handlers, and others do the job as a business. No one category of instructors is any better than another, but experience and ability vary tremendously depending on the individuals concerned. If you cannot get the help you need from your local club, ask around as there might be another more capable or suitable source of help available.

The cost of the benefit of their expertise can vary too, depending on your area, whether you choose to go with a class or privately, and the demand. Quite often the best are a little more expensive because of the demand on their time, but this does not always follow.

For the dog and handler with few vices but a lot to learn, the best place is probably in a class situation with lots of other people in the same predicament. You learn together but at your own pace. Do not be afraid to ask for advice if you are not sure: you may be treated as a class, but good instructors welcome constructive questions, and your class members will more than likely benefit from the

Training class is the ideal place to socialise your dog and learn how to control him in all situations.

If you find that you and your dog take naturally to obedience, you may consider joining an obedience team. Performing here is the Rottweiler Club of Victoria Obedience Team. Photo courtesy of P. Hall.

answers given. If the club you eventually join upsets you in any way, then look elsewhere. Don't be tempted to rough handle your dog just because some ill-informed instructor thinks that it is the only way. Kindness is always the best policy, coupled with good basic understanding—do not be misled.

When looking for a class, make sure that the one you find is for dog obedience and not just ring craft. Good basic control is taught in obedience classes; while ring craft can come later if you want to show your dog in the breed ring.

Many classes do specialise in specific branches of the dog world such as competitive obedience, agility, flyball, working trials, breed showing or demonstrations. If you know that you are particularly interested in any of these aspects, it's worth finding the right club. The national kennel club and dog-specific magazines should be able to help you.

Compulsive Behaviour

Many dogs develop compulsive reactions—they seem to react without knowing what they are doing. Often dogs who are confined to small areas or deprived of toys, play, etc., will develop strange behaviour patterns and stereotypic actions such as pacing and tail chasing (see Unusual Behaviour). Other behaviours that could be termed as compulsive are the products of outside stimuli or even passive training (see Passive Training).

Compulsive behaviour develops because the dog derives either great pleasure or some form of relief or release from the action. For instance, a dog who gets very excited each time he sees a ball and will 'sell his soul' to be retrieving it is a dog who derives great pleasure from the chase, and possibly the kill. Retrieving releases his instincts and allows him to let off steam. Some breeds, particularly working types, will keep going as long as you do, with a seemingly endless supply of drive compelling them to carry on. Some dogs seem compulsive about everything they do: with an un-ending supply of zest, they are not always easy to live with but make excellent working dogs. Others only switch on their compulsive drive when work or play is mentioned.

Whatever the type, it is not an easy one to crack. Should you want to break the habit or calm the dog down, then lots of time and distractive training are the order of the day, together with patience, kindness, thought, and good timing (see Distraction Training, Timing).

Coprophagy

Some dogs, particularly the younger ones, have the distasteful habit of eating things which we humans would rather they didn't, such as wall paper and plaster from the walls, rubbish from the bins, and, most distasteful of all to us humans, their own faeces, or the faeces of other animals including, given the chance, humans.

There is a small chance that a slight adjustment in your dog's diet can remedy this situation. Usually the addition of an additive high in minerals and trace elements, such as seaweed powder (kelp), is the answer. As I say, there is a chance that nutrition is the reason for this behaviour. It is more likely, however, that the behaviour is perfectly natural to the dog, and is something that has to be trained out if you find that you can't live with it.

If the dog just eats its own faeces, there are products available on the retail market that are completely natural and can be added to the dog's food to make the faeces unpalatable to the dog. If he is not so choosy and just anybody's will do, then it's a matter of training: use distraction training and rewards to recondition the dog (see also Reward Training, Leave on Command).

The same training principles for curbing coprophagy apply to eating garbage, wallpaper, etc. Try the supplement of minerals and trace elements, but usually the behaviour has derived from boredom or by the action being rewarded by the very fact that it has been allowed to occur, and thus the dog finds pleasure or release from it, and retraining is the only answer.

Crossing the Road

As a dog owner you are responsible for your dog's actions, especially in a public place. It is advisable to keep your dog on a lead and collar at all times near roads even if the road does not specifically require it. You cannot predict what might startle even the most well-trained dog, and the person responsible for any accident caused by your dog on the road would be you, or whoever was in charge of your dog at the time.

Assuming you have already taught your dog to sit by your side and to walk to heel, you can then introduce him to being 'street wise.' First, it is advisable to introduce him to a quiet road from a distance (with lead and collar on, of course), and then gradually over a period of time bring him nearer to traffic so that he is not frightened or excited by it. After a few days, or maybe a little longer with a timid dog, you will be able to stand with your

Make sure that you have full control before attempting to take your dog across busy roads.

Walk reassuringly and briskly when you are sure that you have plenty of time to do so safely and without frightening your dog.

dog sitting by your side at the edge of the road. The next step is to choose a quiet road. Check that it is very clear, give the command 'heel,' and walk briskly with your dog to the opposite side, and safety. As your dog grows more confident, you will be able to choose busier roads, always making sure that your dog sits quietly by your side until the road is clear and safe to cross. If you take your training step by step, your dog will very soon be able to cross the road with you, without being worried by the traffic passing.

If you have a dog who is frightened of traffic, you will need to follow the procedure already described, spending a long time on the first stages, i.e., on a quiet road with the traffic at a good distance. Don't put the dog in a position where traffic can come from behind and startle him. Keep in control of the situation, and keep calm and reassuring yourself. It can help if you take the dog up to stationary cars or to cars that have their engines running but are not moving, as doing so can help to build confidence if approached very gradually.

Diet

One factor affecting your dog's behaviour is diet. The most effective guide is your dog: watch his weight and activity levels, and adjust your feeding accordingly. Puppies need several smaller meals per day, as do elderly dogs. Adult dogs usually only require one or two good meals per day. Most people prefer to give the single meal, or the larger of the two, in the early evening so that, after being well exercised and trained during the day, the dog can eat his fill, be allowed outside to relieve himself, and then settle down for the night.

Generally, the more activity you require from your dog, the higher protein levels he will need. Often pet dogs who are not required to work all day are given protein levels that far exceed their needs. Excess protein can contribute to hyperactivity in dogs, as can colourants and other additives. Some dogs, like some humans, are more sensitive to these things than others, so it's worth

You must guard against overfeeding your dog from puppyhood. Sometimes dogs want to eat simply because they want to chew, in which case a safe chew such as a Nylabone® can prove ideal.

experimenting with lower protein diets and diets that contain no additives if you have a problem. To lessen the possibility of dietary disorders, it is most important to follow the directions set out by the manufacturer. Sticking to the guidelines lessens the chances of a dietary imbalance of some sort in the dog, and so minimizes the chances of behaviour problems related to food intake.

At the time of writing, I can find no scientific evidence to back the following statement up, but my experience has shown that, for some of my clients, adjustments in diet together with new training programmes have notably calmed their dogs.

Do not be surprised if you need to adjust your dog's diet as he goes through life. Just like yours, his dietary intake level depends upon his age, the type of activity he enjoys, and his general physical make-up.

As I explained at the start, the best guide by far is your dog: watch him, learn to understand him as you would a child, watch his reactions to certain foods, and respond accordingly (see also Energy, Feeding, Hyperactivity).

Proper feeding involves monitoring your dog's appearance and appetite. Taking to his meal with zest, Vizsla photographed by R. Reagan.

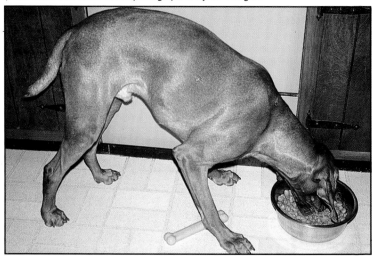

Digging

If we take our pet for a leisurely walk on a deserted beach and he suddenly starts 'digging for gold,' we as humans tend to say, 'Oh look, isn't that cute? Look at him digging.' Take the same dog into your garden with your prized petunias and all of a sudden it isn't so cute. Our poor misunderstood pet. One minute we like his antics, the next we don't. Digging is an instinct that lies deep within him just waiting for an opportunity to burst forth; it is an instinct that serves no real purpose in our modern society and yet often rears its head. Some dogs never feel the need to use this talent, whilst others seem to dig in at every opportunity. Some dogs will bury bones or unwanted food, whilst others seem to dig for the sheer hell of it.

Oscar is most definitely a digger. It seems fateful that those with the most difficult coats to look after have the dirtiest habits!

As I said at the start, often our dogs are encouraged by our amusement of their antics. But, when it becomes a problem, our dogs are then confused by our anger. If you have a gardening enthusiast in the family, it is as well to define which parts of the garden are definitely out of bounds. I like to set aside a part of the garden that is just for the dog, even just a small area is better than nothing. Always encourage the dog to go to this area to defecate or just to have a mooch about, so if he feels the urge to go digging, not too much harm will be done. Teach the dog which areas of the garden are definite 'no-go' areas by taking him around the garden on a lead. If he tries to go onto the areas that you don't want him to, pull him away using the checking action described in the heelwork section, using the command 'off,' and then immediately praise him when he is in the desired place. If you start off by

Terriers, bred for generations to 'go to ground,' are among the finest of diggers in the canine world. Lakeland Terrier owned by A. B. Goldberg photographed by I. Francais.

yelling from the kitchen window each time he goes onto forbidden territory, he will learn nothing except that you are an extremely aggravated person. He may even start to think that he can only gain pleasure by doing certain things in your absence, as when you are not present nothing untoward happens, and indeed he is rewarded by the very act bringing pleasure to him.

So teach him the rules calmly, quietly, and patiently, praising each time he is right, and distracting him to prevent his going wrong.

—————— **Disabilities**

Dogs are most adaptable creatures who can learn to enjoy life with all sorts of disabilities such as blindness, deafness, and even missing limbs. Often these disabilities come in later life, and dogs who have already had some training are easily taught alternative methods such as touch, sound, and hand signals. Dogs who have their disability before or during training are easily taught to use whatever means they have. So long as people make allowances for their disability without being over protective or unrealistic, the dog will progress quite nicely.

DEAFNESS

It's not always easy to remember that a dog is deaf, as there are no outward signs, particularly if deafness comes in later life. You have to remember many things for a deaf dog, such as the fact that he can't hear traffic coming. Even your own car moving in the drive can be a danger to a deaf dog, as he can't hear its engine or your calling. My old dog Guacha is stone deaf, but we often catch ourselves calling to her as she trots off in the opposite direction. You must think ahead to make sure that deaf dogs do not walk into danger.

BLINDNESS

Dogs typically have a little more trouble adjusting to blindness than they do to deafness, but they soon learn to find their way around their own environment, and, with little practice, can move around quite easily. Moving furniture around too often can cause confusion, but, on the whole dogs adjust rapidly. Obviously, precaution must be taken when the dog is on unfamiliar ground.

DEAFNESS AND BLINDNESS

Being both deaf and blind is more often the problem of older dogs than young ones, and because it is typically a gradual

No, dogs don't wear spectacles. But owners can otherwise properly care for the dog with failing eyesight. Photo by R. Pearcy.

dog who was later diagnosed as being deaf and blind. He soon became accustomed to his new surroundings and would run around in the circles that he had investigated and proven safe to run in. He had one very keen sense, the sense of smell. He could smell the farmer's chickens and would rush towards them. They soon learnt that he wasn't a very good shot and would stroll nonchalantly out of the way.

While he was clinically deaf, we found that he could detect the very high pitched sound of a small bell. Together with this bell and strong-smelling liver titbits, we taught him to walk on a lead following the smell and to come back on the sound of the bell, with the treat as an enticement, which was then given to him as a reward, of course. He soon learnt to trust his new owner and live a relatively enjoyable life chasing chickens.

process of deterioration, dogs normally adjust quite well. I have never come across an adult deaf and blind dog who was actually born that way, as most breeders would have such an animal put to sleep as soon as the condition was diagnosed.

I was once called out to a lady who rescued from the middle of a busy road an old

DISABLED OWNERS

As we all know, dogs can be trained to help their disabled owners in many ways: as guide dogs, hearing dogs and as able bodies for the physically handicapped. If you have a handicap, it's best to talk to professionals who can assess your particular needs. If you become disabled whilst you are the owner of a dog—depending on your disabilities and the temperament of your dog—it may be possible to train him to help you. It's best to take professional advice, as each disability has its special needs. You will probably find that a professional dog trainer will be able to help you and will in any case show you how to train the dog to accommodate your particular problems.

Jake is a real Seeing Eye® dog, the product of years of dedicated training.

Distraction Training

To be successful at distraction training, the handler must be keenly aware of his dog at all times: at first sign that the dog is going awry, the handler must appropriately intervene.

Distraction training is most useful in breaking a dog of bad habits, or rather habits that are not in compliance with your rules. For example, distraction training can be employed on the dog who runs barking towards other dogs or people in the park, or the dog who keeps going on to the wrong side of the garden and trampling your prized petunias, or, in fact, the dog who demonstrates any other form of undesirable, compulsive, or unusual behaviour.

The idea behind distraction training is to make something else far more interesting than whatever elicits the problem behaviour.

Following the programme discussed in the play training section, you can teach your dog to be very exuberant and keen on his toy, which can then be used when danger strikes, i.e., just before your dog is about to commit the problem act, you produce his toy, thereby transferring his energy to the toy, and thus *distracting* him.

You need to set up the training situations so that you can be ready to respond, always aware of his strong interests. The secret is to produce your toy before the dog has homed in on his vice, otherwise you may miss your chance as his reaction to his vice will probably be quite compulsive. If he so much as glances in any direction but

The key to distraction training is having something that the dog finds more interesting than anything else, and providing it at opportune times.

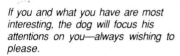

If you and what you have are most interesting, the dog will focus his attentions on you—always wishing to please.

yours, it's up to you to make the game all the more interesting. Don't have the toy out all the time as this will then make it uninteresting and boring. It must be produced fresh and exciting each time there is a need, so creating an exciting distraction. Titbits can also be used in the same way if you are lucky to have a dog whose stomach rules his head.

Top and Bottom: *When your dog takes an overzealous interest in something that he should not—including another dog—simply produce a toy or other object that he has been conditioned to find most interesting, thereby distracting him.*

Once your dog takes interest in your object of distraction, he can easily be led away from the undesirable situation.

Distraction training can be used effectively on all dogs, regardless of their breed.

Dominance

Dominance is probably one of the major reasons why people seek the professional help of a dog trainer. If left to his own devices, a dominant dog will soon have the whole household working around him. His natural instinct, if he were in the wild, would be to strive to become the top dog, or pack leader, and to dictate to the rest of the pack what should happen next. He would eat first, take his pick of the best bitches (or dogs) as his mates, and only allow other dogs to come near him when he wanted them to.

The dog in your home has no reason to suppose that your household situation is any different from that of the wild, unless you educate him to the contrary.

Dominance is a trait that seems to creep up on a family without their noticing, if the daily routine gives the dog increasing feelings of supremacy that goes unnoticed by the human members. Dogs with dominant tendencies will be trying their luck as early as when they are still in the nest (see Adolescence, Young Dogs).

As always with undesirable behaviour, prevention is far easier than cure. If you have a dog who you feel is taking control and starting to dominate your lifestyle, consider the following points very carefully:

1. Does your dog always or usually get fed first?

2. Does your dog growl if you go near his food dish whilst he's eating?

3. Did your dog choose his own sleeping area, and does he grumble if you try to move him?

4. Does your dog get an instant response from you when he asks to go out?

5. Does your dog have his own toys, and do you play when he asks?

6. Do you have difficulty grooming any part of your dog's body?

7. Does your dog object to being physically put into the

down position, or to being handled in any way?

If you have answered 'yes' to some or all of these questions, you must look for ways of reversing your answer. Once a dog starts to become dominant, he usually gets more powerful mentally as he goes along, and it is not a problem that he will grow out of.

Here are some simple rules which you need to abide by to deter your dog from being dominant and to start to condition him to taking a more submissive role:

1. Always make sure that you feed yourself and the rest of your family first, and make sure that the dog is aware that you are doing it.

2. Purchase for your dog toys to play with; but, after having a game with him, put the toys away so that he learns that the toys belong to you and that he is allowed to play only at your discretion. Put the toys safely out of the dog's reach after the

Proper training is one excellent way to assume the role of master, thereby avoiding any possible problems of a dominant dog.

Some breeds, like the Rottweiler, are naturally more dominant than others. It takes a specific kind of person to be a good owner of a dominant dog.

game so that he cannot become possessive over them.

3. If you play with a Gumabone Tug Toy® or similar toy, make sure that the dog does not win every time and take possession of the toy.

4. Adjust your way of thinking to anticipate when your dog will need to relieve himself, and make the decision to take him out. Do not wait until he demands it.

5. Make sure that you can take your dog's food away from him whilst he is eating (see also Aggression, Feeding, Play Training).

All in all it's a case of remembering that you are an intelligent human being. Be aware of a dog's needs for food, play, exercise, love, etc. Make sure that he gets his fair share, but remember that it must be when *you* say, and not when *he* demands.

The most difficult dog I have ever come across was a very dominant, very bored, English Bull Terrier. His story is worth reading in the section on unpredictable behaviour, and it will serve as a model to those who allow their dog to make his own decisions and demands.

Down

Some dogs take to the down position more easily than others. The larger and more dominant breeds, and often the small but strong terrier breeds, sometimes take exception to being made to go into this submissive position. In the down position the dog feels at his most vulnerable. Those people who are battling with a dominant dog will realise that, once the dog starts to accept this position without objection, they are another step on the way to coping with the situation.

The first step when teaching the down is thinking about your command carefully. Employing the word 'down' would seem the most logical, but having already taught your dog that the down command means 'lie down,' do not be surprised if, when he jumps onto your best seat with his muddy paws and you shout, 'Get down,' he lies down on the seat. Well, it is what you told him, isn't it? He is not a mind

Even small dogs can take exception to being made to go into the submissive down position.

reader: 'down' means 'down,' if you are doing your training correctly. So why all of a sudden should it mean 'get off'?

Having sorted in your own mind the actual commands to be used, you can start to teach the down position in association with your chosen command. As always, actions like the down must be taught with the dog under full control, i.e., with a lead and collar on, and in a peaceful environment where the dog does not feel threatened.

Very young puppies can be taught this exercise by gently holding them in front of the shoulders and pushing backwards and downwards—the dog almost hinges backwards and down into the down position. Along with this action say the dog's name and give the command 'down.' Hold the pup there for a few seconds only, repeating gently the command 'down' and praising quietly whilst he is in the correct position. Just a few seconds winning with your pup will prevent months of training and frustration, particularly with the dominant breeds.

Some dogs are very body sensitive and may wriggle and squirm, or turn on their backs. Do not worry about such behaviour. Just calmly and quietly maintain the down position for a few seconds and then release the dog. If he wriggles about, do not add to the fuss by entering into a game either consciously or subconsciously. Think carefully about what you are doing and the dog's response. Keep calm, methodical, and meaningful

without being harsh or aggressive in your manner, and handle him as little as possible. If you do show aggression in your manner, no matter how slight, the dog's response will be to jump up and say he's sorry for whatever it was that he has done 'wrong,' and he won't even understand what it is that he is apologising for . Aggression teaches nothing but fear, apprehension, and sometimes a retaliation of aggression.

The dog must understand that you are the one who put him into the down position. He must also be aware of the fact that you release him. He may try to change positions, e.g., to sit or stand, which may not seem particularly important to you (you may have been about to release him anyway), but do not allow the dog to make this decision for himself. The whole essence of dog training is teaching the dog to obey commands. If you allow him sometimes to make his own decisions following a command, he will very soon learn that your commands mean nothing. If the dog does break the position, immediately place him physically but gently back in the correct position, thus maintaining your control and command of the situation—in the nicest possible way, of course.

With a large dog it is often useful to use his own weight to your advantage. With the dog on a short lead, place him in the sit position on your left side; encourage him, by applying gentle pressure on his shoulder, to push towards you. When you start to feel sufficient push coming your way, release your pressure and snatch the lead downwards and towards you, at the same time giving the command 'down.' In this way, you use the dog's own weight to help you get him into the down position. The technique requires a little practice but, once perfected, can reduce what might seem like a difficult task to quite an easy one.

If you have a sensitive, gentle hand you may be able to find your dog's pressure points. This sounds a little bizarre I know, but every dog has them. Gentle exploring around the region of the front of the chest, just below the neck, will reveal two little indentations. *Very*

gentle pressure applied to this area on a relaxed dog will simply make the dog flop down. Again, it is not the easiest of techniques, but an interesting one worth exploring when you are having a quiet moment with your dog.

The technique that will probably suit most handlers is as follows: Start with your dog in the sit position on your left

Given time, patience, and good technique, this feisty little dog became comfortable in the down position.

side, and on a short lead; push the dog to the side and downwards with your left hand and pull the lead down towards the ground with your right hand, at the same time giving your verbal commands. You may find it easier to push the dog down with your left hand, while at the same time sweeping his front feet forwards. All depends on you and the dog: choose a method with which you feel comfortable, so long as the end result is that the dog is in the down position comfortably and happily. The most important thing to remember is to command and encourage the dog as he goes into the down, and give gentle praise once he is there. If you lose control or he jumps up, simply start all over again. Do not be defeated, and do not be lulled into thinking, 'Well he had enough anyway, so I'll let it go this time.' Doing so merely teaches the dog that 'down' means 'do as you like.'

If you have difficulty getting your dog into the down position, please do not give up, and, if necessary, seek professional advice to help you master this important exercise. There is a slight possibility that the dog could have some physical problem that makes it painful for him to be put into the down position. If in doubt, check with your vet.

Once you have mastered the technique of getting your dog down, and he starts to relax, you can very gradually begin to lengthen the time that the dog stays in the position.

Take it very gradually, reassuring the dog that he is correct by repeating the down command and giving gentle praise. Avoid suddenly using his name whilst he is down, as he may become confused and think that you want him to come to you. Any use of his name should be calmly and quietly administered, with no sudden or excitable tones that could induce him into jumping up.

Dogs can be taught the down by using a titbit as a lure. Let the dog know you have it, then lower your hand to the floor giving the command 'down,' releasing the titbit when the dog is in the down position. He may take a few moments to realise what you want, but do

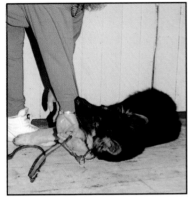

Dogs may struggle a bit and even nip at the handler's sleeve if they resent being put in the down position.

not release the titbit until he is down. This method can save a lot of wriggling and handling, but be careful not to allow the dog to spring up as soon as he has eaten the titbit.

If your dog should growl or show any aggression when you try to teach this exercise, read the sections on dominance and aggression before proceeding.

Finally, do not forget that the all-important factor to teaching any exercise is timing. Incorrect timing leads to confusion. If you have not already done so, or to refresh your memory, turn to the section on timing.

Pulling down from the neck does not portray to the dog what is required, and he will merely look down or pull against you.

Eating Grass ────

The subject of a dog's eating grass has been studied widely, yet why dogs do it has not been scientifically proven. Cats eat grass to add folic acid to their diets; dogs eat grass and then often vomit what they have eaten, although some grass does go through the digestive system. I have noticed that dogs often eat grass when under stress or when thirsty. Whatever the reason, it seems a normal reaction for dogs, and, with something of this nature, it is probably as well to allow it to take its course, so long as the behaviour does not become an obsession. On occasions, dogs have become almost compulsive grass eaters, but it is possible to stop this behaviour by following simple training procedures (see Training), and it would be sensible to have your dog checked by the vet in case there is some digestive disorder.

Energy

Working sledge pullers like the Siberian Husky are bred for endurance, thus they have abounding energy that needs outlet. Photo courtesy of J. Russell, breeder, driver.

The dog's energy level depends on many factors, including breeding, feeding, exercise routine, and others.

EXCESSIVE ENERGY

Just like some people, some dogs are naturally more active and energetic than others— athletic parents tend to produce athletic offspring. Those of us who follow a sensible eating programme with the correct balance of nutrients, calories, vitamins, etc., have far more energy than those who eat high-fat, high-calorie diets; and those who follow an active routine with adequate exercise, etc., are always ready for more. Some chemicals such as artificial colourings, additives, etc., can affect humans and cause hyperactivity, and it is possible that these could have the same effect on dogs (see Diet).

I have been called out on numerous occasions to distressed owners whose dogs are often so full of energy that they are unbearable. Almost without exception these dogs are members of working breeds, e.g., various gundogs, sheepdogs, and terriers, Labradors and Golden Retrievers at the top of the list (probably due to their popularity as opposed to their having any more energy reserves than other working breeds). (See also Hyperactivity.)

Owners often vastly underestimate the amount of exercise and training needed for many dogs to use up their energy. These dogs have often been bred to keep going all day,

and, when placed into a household situation, find it very difficult to expend all of that energy on just a few miles of walking or even free exercise each day (see also Working Dogs).

Many people reading this will not have the choice of rethinking their decision on selecting their breed, and so a solution to excessive energy must be found.

Very careful thought should be given to the diet of your dog. It is important to follow the manufacturer's guidelines to the letter. Do not feed a working-dog-type diet to your pet just because he is a working breed. Food does not read pedigrees; it only provides energy to carry out tasks. If you feed a working-dog diet to the common house dog, you will be giving the dog sufficient energy to work all day but insufficient access to expend that energy.

Training is better than exercise in the using up of energy: think how tired you become when having to concentrate for any length of time—far more tired than if you were working out at the gym. So a training session as part of

The Rottweiler is truly a working dog, and his abounding energy can be well directed to obedience and other tasks.

beneficial in more ways than one. It's often a good idea to let your pet have some freedom in the garden or his own special area so that he can let off steam—and not be under your feet, which helps to give both dog and owner some freedom. The garden or other run is also a place where the dog can always be put if he is particularly active and you are not in a position to take him for a run or occupy him immediately. Even a training session in the lounge or garden, going through the routines or teaching something new, will help your dog to use up his energy. But remember to make it interesting and keep it fun.

LACK OF ENERGY

When your dog is lethargic, it is important to analyse his condition and environment. If he is always lacklustre, then a visit to the vet is advisable. If the vet gives you the all-clear, then consider the dog's diet. Is it sufficiently high in protein for the dog's type and activity level? (See diet.) If your dog is lacking in energy only at certain times, try to isolate specific factors that occur both before those times and during them, and take note of them.

Often at shows I hear handlers complaining that their dogs have no energy and will ask if there is something that they can give to them, some pill or potion that will pep them up. Often this lack of energy, when it boils down to the real reason,

Taking time out for warm praise and kind words helps to keep the dog happy and motivated.

is confusion or lack of motivation. Some of the things that we ask of our dogs must seem very foolish and unnecessary to them. We ask them to stand in a certain posture in the breed ring or to walk with such repetitive accuracy in obedience classes that any intelligent being would get bored and lacklustre in his performance. Often these animals, given a change of scenery, a ball to chase, some delicious food, a nice bitch for a dog, or a corn field to romp in, would exhibit a different character altogether, one full of energy and zest for life.

If your dog's energy level can switch on and off, then motivation is more likely the problem, not lack of energy (see Motivation). If you have checked with your vet and been given the all-clear, and yet your dog still does not enjoy life, either all the time or at certain times, analyse his daily routine. Do you require him to work after he has been engaged in some compulsive or abnormal behaviour? If he is kenneled, does he pace or throw himself around, displaying stereotypic behaviour? Try changing his

Dogs respond to their environment: introducing a zesty youngster to a poorly motivated dog can renew his vigor.

daily routine. Give him a change of scenery. Try extra vitamins and minerals. Teach him to play following the play-training routine (see Play Training). If he has good days and bad days, think carefully about what may have happened to make him lethargic. Observe his every mood, as you could find the answer on your doorstep. Motivate him. Play with him. Be his friend.

Equipment

What is needed to train your dog?

In England the law states that your dog must wear some form of identification holder with your name and your address clearly written on or engraved in it, with an engraved disc being the more durable.

On acquiring a new puppy, most of us rush off to the nearest pet shop and buy everything we think we need, and often come back with the things that the shopkeeper thinks we need, too. Think carefully and you could save yourself a lot of money.

First, your new pet needs a place to call his own. The best type of proprietary beds are the solid plastic ones. Other types of beds, although they may look great, can bring problems if your new puppy turns out to be a chewer. Can you imagine what it's like when a dog chews a hole in a bean bag for instance? It's amazing how far white polystyrene beads can go!

Wicker baskets look great, particularly if you like cane furniture, but they are quite difficult to keep clean, with all those cracks and crevices, and again are quite interesting to chew from a canine point of view. If you are handy with a hammer and nails, you can soon knock up a wooden bed, but, as a general rule of thumb, what you can build can usually be purchased for less money, not to mention less time.

As for bedding, the best type available is the veterinary type, which was originally designed for use in hospitals. It is very soft and warm, and any 'spillages' go straight through, keeping the dog dry. It is relatively uninteresting to chew—most dogs do not bother—however, there is always the exception!

As for collars and leads, a soft fabric or leather buckled collar is the best start for young pups. The lead should have a trigger-style clip to be safe and should be made of soft but

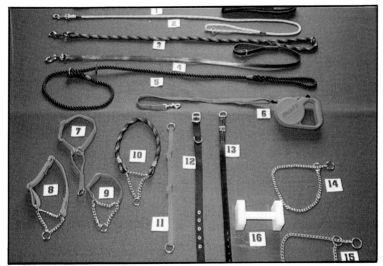

Equipment: 1. strong yet soft webbing lead; 2 and 3. soft rope leads; 4. soft bridle lead; (1–4 all have safe trigger and hook fasteners, and the ring in the handle can be used to shorten the lead or to clip it around your body when the dog is loose); 5. gundog-style lead with stopper that fixes the collar in position; 6. the extending lead to give your dog more freedom whilst keeping complete control; 7,8,9, and 10. various types of half check collars (these are not as harsh as a check chain); 11. the fitted and adjustable slip collar; 12 and 13. soft webbing or leather collars; 14 and 15. check chains; 16. competition-style dumbbell.

strong fabric, such as cotton webbing, rope, or bridle leather. I personally do not find chain leads comfortable when training. Check chains or choke chains are not necessary for young dogs. In fact, if you follow the techniques in this book, you will never need one. With strong dogs they can make training easier, but only if used carefully, thoughtfully, and correctly.

On the rare occasions when I

To be effective at all, the collar must fit properly. Photo by I. Francais of Japanese Chin owned by P. Mannes and J. DeMenna.

use a check collar, I prefer to go for an all-in-one gundog-style lead and collar combined, which is made from rope and has a rubber or leather stop so that you can position the collar high on the dog's neck for the best effect, and the dog cannot back out. Even with a very strong dog, just a twist of the wrist is all that is needed to bring him back to heel, if you follow the procedures and techniques correctly.

There are also a number of halter-style or head collars available. These are a useful aid to stop a dog from pulling, although in themselves they teach the dog nothing. Just like when using any other collar, it's the handler who must train the dog. Not everyone likes the appearance of head collars, and they are often mistaken for muzzles. In fact, they will close the dog's mouth when checked, but they can be invaluable to gain control, particularly if you are unable to train your dog or if you have some disability that makes training difficult for you. If you are re-training an aggressive dog then a correctly fitted head collar will act as a muzzle and so prevent any accidents.

Some schools recommend the use of spiked and/or electric collars. To my mind they are totally barbaric. A trainer who cannot train a dog without them is in the wrong business. Kindness and understanding, coupled with good timing and technique, will teach any healthy dog to be an acceptable member of the community.

Fitted slip collars are a useful aid in controlling a powerful dog because they stay in position high on the neck. Care should be taken if these are used on a growing dog. If the collar is not adjustable, it

With proper equipment and correct technique, even youngsters can skilfully train a dog.

Grooming tables are a must for owners who show their dogs, particularly if the breed requires extensive show-ring preparation. Komondor photographed by I. Francais.

pressure on swollen glands. In any case they are not necessary for younger or small dogs.

Toys are another essential part of your dog training equipment, but they must be safe (see Toys). Dogs, like children, learn through play. The use of toys in moulding and shaping the dog's behaviour can produce magnificent results.

Grooming is an important social event in the canine family, and owners of long- and short-coated dogs should make it a daily event for both man and dog to enjoy. There are masses of different types of brushes and combs on the market. Choose one that is suitable for your dog's coat.

It is surprising how many people find it difficult to handle their adult dogs. If they had regular grooming sessions of all parts of the dog's body, handling would have become quite the normal thing to do; and, should the need arise, following injury or skin infection, the dog would have no objections to being handled, making correct diagnosis and treatment so much easier (see Grooming).

will soon be too small and the dog could be most uncomfortable and would learn nothing. These collars should not be used on dogs who are teething, as they could put

Excitement

Most problems involving excitement are caused by the dog's going 'over the top' or getting 'too wound up'—he hurtles 'round in circles, barks, jumps on the furniture, and causes other havoc.

An excitable dog is a pleasure to work with—once you understand the doggy mind—because you can channel that excitement, that energy, that joy of life, into whatever you want from your dog. It is no use trying to push an excitable dog down or 'keep him under' because sooner or later his character will come bubbling out. Many people who do competition work would give their right arm for an excitable dog, as placid types are much more difficult to motivate.

In the household situation, excitable dogs take a bit of getting used to. They come into your quiet abode, often as a playful puppy, and as they get larger they become more playful until somehow even the smallest dog seems larger than

An excitable dog can be a pleasure to work with once you have taught him the basic ground rules by which he must live. Make sure that you give him something to focus his excitement on— regular training sessions with lots of fun.

Yearning to enter the ring, this Kerry Blue Terrier abounds with excitement. Photo by I. Francais of Kerry owned by R. Thompson.

life. It is as well to have an area where your excitable dog can go when you want some time to yourself, a kennel and run are ideal (see Kennels) or if space is a problem, a cage or crate.

Most importantly, you should set about teaching him all of the control commands, such as sit, down, come back, speak on command (and so, 'quiet'), heel, and others. The more you teach your dog, the easier he will be to live with and the more you will be able to enjoy his presence instead of resenting it. Learn to understand when your dog reacts to certain situations and make sure that you are in control of him before he reacts. Don't wait for things to go wrong. The more positive your responses, the less of a problem and the more of a joy and a talking point your canine friend will be.

Use the things that you have taught your dog to keep in control of situations. Train on a regular basis to refresh your dog's and your own responses so that excitement does not blot out the teaching and allow instinct to take over.

Exercise

The amount of exercise that your dog needs varies with the breed, as well as the individual dog. Some dogs, particularly working breeds, have been selectively bred over generations for stamina.

Problems arise when these dogs are expected to fit into a household situation. Ninety percent of the problem dogs whom I am called out to see have problems that stem from being very active, and nearly all of these 90% are Labrador Retriever or Golden Retriever

Working breeds can keep going all day, and they need mental stimulation as well as exercise to keep them happy and controlled.

types—the two breed types that are seen by the public as the docile, intelligent companions of the blind and the gentle puppies from TV advertisements.

Guide dogs are almost always bred by the Guide Dogs For The Blind Association, from their own bloodlines, and are often the results of first crosses. They also go through very extensive training over a period of two years, which is far more training than any pet dog is likely to get in his lifetime. A few years ago, my husband and I were invited to the G.D.F.T.B. Training Centre at Leamington Spa, England, and enjoyed looking around the kennels and training facilities. We also had the privilege of being led with our eyes closed by a trained guide dog who was at the centre for a refresher course. He skilfully guided us through the busy streets of Leamington. What an experience that was for a sighted person. We later used that knowledge to design a new harness to help make life easier for the blind people and their guide dogs. I digress. Back to exercise.

Obviously the amount of exercise required varies so much from dog to dog, but I am a firm believer in putting my dogs through a little training programme each day—similar to going through a daily keep-fit programme for humans. It helps the body stay trim and also keeps the mind in tune. A dog who enjoys a constructive training session every day, coupled with some free exercise, will become a pleasure to own. By combining free play and training, you exercise not only his body but also his brain. The more we teach our dogs, the more they are capable of learning. The easier they find it to learn, the easier they are to control. It all blends together to make sharing your life with a dog a real pleasure.

Small dogs also need good quality exercise to keep them fit and healthy. Often owners leave toy breeds to run around the garden and neglect to take them out. These dogs may well derive sufficient exercise in the garden if they are the active type who runs around for the sheer fun of it, but still they do not receive the social aspect of being exercised in varying environments and may well not

Labradors are typically very active dogs. Having a good game of fetch really exercises their instinct to retrieve.

develop the social skills that help them to cope with the big, wide world. It is important for all breeds to get out with their owners, not only to keep fit physically but to become mentally well adjusted, too.

Fearfulness

I believe that a dog's temperament is determined roughly 25% by his breeding (genetics) and 75% by his up-bringing (environment). Like human babies, puppies are very vulnerable. Up to around twenty weeks of age, puppies experience what we might call their critical period. Everything that happens to the pup during this critical period of learning has an effect on how he will cope with life later on. Fortunately most of us muddle through without causing too much trauma in the dog, but, occasionally something happens to a pup that frightens him, and he then comes to associate this fear with some of the things that we would consider as part of everyday life. Puppies can be frightened by something that is part of our daily life, and yet we can be quite unaware that it has happened.

Usually, by observing the pup's reactions to various situations, we can start to understand the possible causes of those reactions. We might not always know the exact reason for the fear, but, by careful handling and observation, we can help the pup to overcome his problems. Before tackling any situation of this nature, you must first gain your dog's confidence by being kind, playful, gentle, and trustworthy.

Teaching your dog to play with you can be a great help in distracting him from the things that frighten him (see Playing). Approach situations that frighten your dog very carefully and from a distance. Do not thrust your dog into a frightening situation, hoping that you will kill or cure. The dog will probably panic and lose his trust in you. So tread carefully, instilling confidence as you go, and use a toy or some other device that the dog enjoys to stop situations from becoming too intense.

Never be tempted to chastise a timid dog in the belief that it will bring him to his senses; it will only serve to make him frightened of you, too.

If you take a child to the dentist, you do not reprimand him for being nervous. It is better to change the subject and talk about something enjoyable, bring out a favourite toy, or tell him a funny story. If a child is frightened of the dark, you don't tell him horror stories, or tell him that you are scared, too. You show him interesting things about the dark, like the stars. I cured my young son's fear of the dark by taking him into the dark armed with a torch. We sat quietly looking at the stars, and then turned the torch across the fields trying to spot rabbits. We didn't see one rabbit but we had a great evening together. Now he can't wait for the dark and a nice clear sky to have fun.

The same applies to your dog. Whatever his fear, you can take away its intensity by being inventive and showing him that there is some fun to be found in every situation.

If your dog runs and hides when someone comes to your door, the best path to take is

Fearfulness should not be confused with the dog's saying 'Back off.' This canine guardian is not afraid but clearly giving a warning. Photo courtesy of L. Burke.

ignoring it. If you rush over and soothe him, or pick him up and try to console him, all you are

If threat display is not enough, the well-trained guard dog will fearlessly do what he must to thwart the adversary. Fearful dogs bark/bite and run the other way.

really doing is rewarding him for his behaviour. If you call him to you, and he does not come, he has received the reward that he wanted, namely to stay hidden, and so you reinforce the problem. The dog should never be forced to approach someone who frightens him, as this can lead to your inadvertently teaching him to snap or bite. A frightened animal follows the fight-or-flight instinct. If you prevent him from running away, you leave him only one option, namely to bite. Your immediate reaction to his aggression is to pull him back to your side, which is the perfect reward in his eyes. He will learn that to prevent being forced to approach a fearful situation is to act aggressively. It is better to allow the dog to build up confidence gradually on his own by putting him in non-stressful situations, allowing strangers to give him his food when he is hungry, and by keeping yourself cool, calm and collected and not becoming caught up in situations that you know frighten your dog.

Feeding

Regular patterns should be set and maintained as much as possible so that your dog's digestive system can form some sort of regularity. If your dog eats too much, particularly late in the day, he may have difficulty in getting through the night without an accident.

Make sure that the type of food you give your dog is suitable to his age, type, and

Be sure that you can handle your dog's food without his feeling threatened—the dog should see you as the source and not a thief of his nourishment.

work load. For instance, young pups need little and often, as do elderly dogs. Be guided by your breeder or vet as to volume and type of food necessary. It really is a matter of seeing what is available in

Feed your dog after the family has eaten to prevent him from adopting the 'top dog' attitude.

your area, and seeking the advice of an expert on your particular breed.

My job is to make sure that your dog's feeding behaviour is correct. The perfectly behaved dog will not pester for food at the dinner table, nor will he growl when people approach him when he is eating. So as soon as you acquire your dog, begin proper training. Always place all of the food for the dog in his own bowl, and do not throw scraps and titbits to him whilst you or your family are eating. Place his feeding bowl out in the open, not in a cosy corner which is easy to protect,

and stay with your dog whilst he is eating.

Your dog must *not* be informed that he is top dog by receiving his food before the rest of the pack (family), as it can lead to dominance and aggression problems.

On a regular basis, make sure that your dog readily accepts your taking away his food whilst he is eating his meal. The best thing to do is to take away his bowl and add a tasty titbit so that he comes to think that, when humans touch his bowl, there is a possibility of something extra.

If you follow these simple rules from the start, problems should not occur. If you already have problems and are not able to go near or attempt to take away the dog's food without his growling or snapping, then turn to the section on aggression over food (see also Diet).

Fighting

Dogs fight for various reasons, usually because they are protecting their domain. Male dogs often squabble but are less likely to come to actual physical harm than bitches. Most dogs, when left to their own devices, will establish harmony with only a few arguments and then settle down to live together. Occasionally, a violent fight can arise when introducing a new dog or re-uniting dogs after a separation (even a short one). Some fights are very difficult to stop; but, if you are ultimately in charge of the pack, loud verbal commands should stop any fight.

In the fights that I have witnessed, I have always been the one to stop them, because the owners of the dogs involved tended to panic, and their voices came out high pitched and hysterical and seemed to add to the frenzy. When a fight starts, I grab whatever is handy—such as a large sweeping brush, a notice board, or a heavy stick—and approach yelling in a very authoritative manner. The object that I grab is not used to hit the dogs but is put between them to catch their attention long enough for my authority to take over. Never put your own hand or arms in, even to try to pull your own dog off, as you are likely to get bitten in the commotion, although accidentally, and even possibly by your own dog. Hose pipes turned on dogs or buckets of water thrown would probably work, but they never seem to be handy at the right time.

As with other problems, avoidance and distraction are far better than having to break up the actual act. Each time dogs fight, the action itself is reinforced, and thus more likely to occur the next time there is a hostile atmosphere.

Presently I have eleven dogs of my own. The only fights that have occurred with my animals have been in my absence, i.e., under the control of someone

When introducing any two strange dogs, be sure to have them securely on a lead, but do not show tension or fear, which will give the dogs reason to think that something is wrong.

else. Personally I can take out all eleven and exercise them as a pack, but I would not risk it with anyone else, as I could not guarantee that person's absolute control as top dog. Some of my dogs can be rather excitable, as they are from varied backgrounds, and are all very individual characters.

Bringing in a young dog to live with your older one usually works if the dogs are allowed to establish their own grounds and hierarchy, if necessary. So long as things don't get out of hand and you remain ultimately in charge, give preference to the older or dominant dog, but let neither dog get the upper hand on you. If the young dog pesters too

If matters get a little heated, be quick to separate the two. When things cool down, the dogs can be re-introduced to one another. Remember to keep relaxed and use your commands and play to call the dog away before things heat up. Thus the dog receives praise for his good behaviour. Photos by I. Francais of Boxers owned by Rick Tomita.

long, the older one will eventually tell him that he's had enough, and the younger one will thereby learn how far he can go.

The importance of socialising cannot be over emphasised when bearing in mind that, even if you only have one dog now, your dog may one day have to accept another. So take every opportunity to develop this important social skill (see Socialisation).

Grooming

All dogs need some grooming, some of course a lot more than others. If you like to work with long hair and also have some spare time after your other doggie duties, then long-haired dogs are great. They need thorough daily grooming. If you do not intend to show your dog, he may look cute with his hair clipped shorter. We keep Oscar's hair shorter than it would naturally be to help keep it in good condition and to keep us from worrying too much if he wants to roll and play outside. Medium- and short-haired breeds are much easier to maintain: a gentle groom once or twice a week is usually sufficient, more if you have been walking in the woods where the dog can pick up bits of debris in his coat. Even with a short-coated dog, daily brushing is a good idea. Not only will it give him a really tip-top look but it will teach him to readily accept being handled. So many owners of such breeds

as the Dobermann, Rottweiler, Labrador Retriever, seem not to think it necessary to groom. In a pack situation, daily grooming would take place as part of the social behaviour. Owners would benefit from mimicking this behaviour, particularly with the larger, more dominant breeds, as the dog will learn to accept handling from his owner and be less likely to try to be dominant over them.

I teach my dogs to enjoy grooming from when they are tiny pups. I use a soft brush to gently groom their soft fur. They soon become accustomed to handling. I check their ears, look at their feet, and generally make sure that everything is as it should be. They soon learn to

Facing page:
All dogs should be taught to accept grooming of all body parts, which is often neglected with short-coated breeds like Rottweilers, Bull Terriers and others.

If you have a long-coated breed and do not have much time for grooming sessions, it may be more practical to have your dog clipped short like Oscar here.

stand still and enjoy the experience, and they never resent being touched if treated with care and understanding.

Some breeds require more specialist grooming and trimming so it's best to go along to a canine beautician, or ask for your breeder's help. If you watch them carefully, you can probably have a go yourself, but you will need to invest in the right sort of equipment. If you want a really neat job, it is best to leave it to the experts.

Guarding

Often when my phone rings, the person on the other end wants their dog to be a guard dog, either to attack on command, or sometimes just to bark on command.

A dog who is trained to attack can be a lethal weapon. I would not teach a dog attack work unless the dog was of a very stable character, and, more importantly, the handler and anyone else who had access to that dog knew exactly what makes a dog tick and how to handle heated situations. In England, as in other countries, there are strict laws governing the ownership of a guard dog. If someone unlawfully entered your property and was attacked by your dog, you can be held liable and likely prosecuted for having a dangerous dog. Even if the intruder had no right to be there and even if he stole some of your possessions, you can still be held liable. So owning a guard dog is not as simple as you think.

I will not explain attack-dog training in a book because I feel that it would be very irresponsible on my part. If you are interested in this sort of work, then my advice is to find a good professional instructor who will evaluate you and your dog as to your suitability and who will guide you every step of the way. Also line up the services of a good lawyer and insurance company, just in case; and, last but not least whatever your instructor might say, teach the dog to stand off (to not attack) *before* you teach him to attack.

Teaching the dog to speak is more easily coped with (see Speak on Command) and can be a most useful deterrent to ward off unwanted guests, and also very rewarding as a display of control.

Housetraining———

We must realise that a young puppy or nervous dog will find it very difficult to go through a whole night without the odd accident.

I prefer to teach my dogs when they are very young to go to the toilet on old newspaper. Most breeders will have used newspaper in the whelping pen, and so pups start to come to associate the newspaper with the correct place to go. Normally it is an easy progression when you get your pup home to put some old newspaper down in an obvious place for him to go. Remember to provide plenty of paper, as pups often go over to the paper and, with all good intentions, put their front feet on but do not realise that the back end is hanging over the edge! Please do not chastise the pup if this happens, as he really does think he is right, and harsh words only confuse him.

A plastic sheet under the paper will protect your carpet. Make sure that there are no faint traces of urine smell on the carpet for the pup to associate with being a place used-before–so-why-not-again, even if the papers are not there. If the plastic sheet is larger than the newspaper, it will save your carpet from spills and accidents.

Each time the pup shows signs of wanting to relieve himself (they tend to sniff around, or start to go around in circles), take him over to the paper and give him a command that means relieve yourself, such as 'be quick' or whatever command you feel comfortable with, as long as you choose a command and stick to it. As the pup relieves himself, you should keep repeating the command, 'Be quick; good boy.' If this command is repeated each time he wants to go, he will by gradual progression learn the command and with what to associate it.

Gradually the paper can be moved towards the door (only move its position when the pup

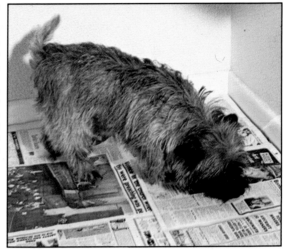

Dogs are naturally clean animals, and thus quite easy to housetrain. It must be remembered, though, that dogs do not gain full control of their bladders and bowels until about three months of age. Photo by S. A. Thompson.

is really confident and positive about where he is going). The aim is eventually to leave the door open with the paper just outside. Then, once the pup is sure of where the paper is, the door can be closed. The pup will probably stand at the door, and may even whimper or bark to be let out. This stage is very crucial, so watch the pup carefully and anticipate when he will need to go. Do not allow him to stand too long at the door as he may give in to the call of nature quicker than you think. Give him every help possible to make sure that he

gets it right every time. Remember that the fewer times he is allowed to do things that are undesirable to you, the more chance he has of understanding how to behave to make you happy. By allowing incorrect actions to occur, you are inadvertently condoning the very action—at least that is how the dog sees it. You can—and many people do—teach your dog to go outside from the very start; however, night time may pose a problem. Unless your pup is allowed access to the outside when he needs it, he will most probably have an accident; and, as I explained before, the more times he is allowed to make mistakes, the more those mistakes are likely to become the norm. A cage or indoor kennel is ideal for helping with housetraining, as a dog will have to be pretty desperate to foul in his own sleeping area.

OLDER DOGS

Occasionally an older dog will start to make the odd mistake in the house; and, if this is not rectified quickly, the dog soon comes to believe that it must be an acceptable thing to do, and thus a problem establishes itself.

The first time your adult dog makes a mistake, you must ask yourself, 'Why?' Did you feed him anything that was different from his normal diet? Did your daily routine differ in any way? Did you forget to give him his final freedom of the evening before retiring to bed? Did something happen in the night to frighten or disturb him? If you can honestly answer 'No' to all of these questions, then it's probably just that odd mistake and no real cause for worry. If your routine or feeding was

different, then correct it the following day if possible, and normally the dog will be as good as gold the next night. If the dog has another accident the next night, then it's as well to have him checked by the vet. He could be suffering from a mild stomach upset or infection.

As dogs progress in years, their bodies begin to degenerate. Sometimes arrangements have to be made so that the dog is able to relieve himself at night if necessary.

I was once called out to a household whose members were at their wits' end with their 18-month-old springer spaniel. He was reversing up to the kitchen units at night and aiming his faeces up the doors and walls, etc. I could not believe my ears. When I arrived at the poor misinformed owners' home, they told me that they had paper trained their dog, and one night he had gone to toilet on his paper but must have been too near to the wall and the mess went all over the wall. (Like I said, dogs do not always realise what the back end is doing!)

So the following evening the

owners prepared to retire for the night by taping newspapers to the kitchen units, and up the walls (forgot the floor). During the night this extremely intelligent springer did a balancing act and emptied himself up the walls.

This went on until the whole of the kitchen units were taped up with newspaper every night, and then the owners decided it was getting a bit beyond a joke, and called for my help.

An 18-month-old healthy dog has no real need to relieve himself during the night, so we devised a new training programme. We took down all the newspaper from the units, and arranged his exercise, feeding and training programme so that he was not uncomfortable or restless by night time. We found that the owners had a quiet outhouse attached to the house which the dog enjoyed being in—so we made him a bed in there. He was allowed to run in and out of the outhouse during the day, and a piece of newspaper was put outside for him to associate it with the act of relieving himself. He went all through the first night without fouling,

If one prefers not to use papers, Wee-Wee Pads[*] can be employed with good results. Photo by I. Francais.

and has never disgraced himself since.

What the owners had done was effectively to train him to go wherever there was newspaper. It sounds funny now but was a very serious problem to them (see Passive Training).

It is most undesirable and unhealthy to have dog faeces in the wrong places—parks, beaches, and pavements would all be more pleasant places to be if dog owners would teach their dogs 'to go' on command in the appropriate place, and then clear it up right after.

Howling

Howling is not quite so common in domestic dogs as it is in the wild. It is usually heard when a dog has been isolated from the family and it basically means 'I'm here, come for me.'

Dogs are instinctively pack animals, and they find it difficult to adjust to isolation.

Most commonly dogs howl when their owner leaves them, and this behaviour can be heightened if, in the same vicinity, there are bitches in heat. The same procedure as the one for barking in the owner's absence can be followed for stopping this behaviour, although sometimes it is a little more difficult if the dog only howls now and again. Choose times for training when the dog might be vulnerable, and teach him to be happy when left in a room on his own. (Follow the training programme set out in the section on barking.)

Dogs howl most commonly when they are separated from their owners—and some dogs will do anything to be reunited with them. Photo by V. Serbin.

Hyperactivity

Hyperactivity must not be confused with abundant energy. A dog who exhibits 'hyperactivity' may simply be in need of exercise. These Jack Russell Terriers demonstrate a fine use of doggie energy. Photo courtesy of Hollow Terriers.

Many factors can lead to hyperactivity. In many cases, the hyperactive dog is of a breed that has been selectively bred for a certain task over many years. He is then bought by a well-meaning individual and expected to live a relatively sedentary existence. OK, most of these pets are walked once or twice a day, but many working dogs have been developed to work *all* of the day. These dogs can settle into a slower pace of life provided they are given lots to occupy the brain, and I mean lots! You will need plenty of time and patience if you want to take on a lively breed.

Some breeds that have been selectively bred for the show ring also have a very lively and often difficult character to control. This quality may be restricted to particular strains within the breed, and it's as well to find out as much as you can about the background breeding before purchasing a puppy. A responsible breeder will help you all he can with particular behavioural traits common to his breed lines. All physically and mentally fit dogs are capable of learning simple obedience lessons which will help you to control them. Additionally, start training as soon as possible—even before obedience class—to prevent bad habits from forming. Some people are convinced that their dog is hyperactive when really it is just a lively, misunderstood individual. Hyperactivity is often a word that is used in desperation as an answer to other problems. So think carefully before deciding that your dog should be labelled hyperactive.

Feeding an unbalanced diet can be a contributory factor so always follow the manufacturer's instructions for feeding very carefully, and feed accordingly. A pet dog does not need a working-dog diet just because he happens to be a working-dog breed! The protein level will be far too high, so be advised by the packaging and/or the breeder, and do not be tempted to add extras to a scientifically produced, balanced diet, unless advised by the vet.

N.b. It has been reported that certain artificial colourants and other additives in a dog's diet can lead to behavioural disturbances such as

Obedience training helps direct your dog's energy to productive ends. Photo by I. Francais of Japanese Chin owned by P. Mannes and J. DeMenna.

hyperactivity. In my experience, as long as you stick to a good quality balanced diet (and there are diets available which contain no additives if you are concerned), follow the manufacturer's advice on feeding, then most dogs are OK. I must stress that it is most important that you do follow the directions, even to the point of weighing the portion to be fed, and make sure that the food you are feeding is suitable for the type of dog you have and his lifestyle (see also Diet, Energy, Unusual Behaviour, Working Dogs, Young Dogs).

Inoculation

After acquiring your dog, your first stop should be the veterinary surgeon, who will make sure that your new dog is fit and give him all relevant injections. Vet in this photo is Mr. D.J. Calvert of Calvert and Aldren Vet.

All dogs should be inoculated against diseases that can cause pain, suffering or even death to themselves or us. On acquiring your pet, before taking him out into public areas, you should take him to the vet who will advise you on all of the inoculations and incubation periods necessary for your geographical area. Do not take your dog out into the streets or public areas until he is fully inoculated and through the necessary incubation period.

This early vet visit will also give the doctor a chance to get to know your pet and check him over to make sure he is in perfect health.

It's also a good time to ask about training classes in your area. Many veterinarians and/or their assistants will know the local clubs, and it's as well to get your name down as soon as possible, as good clubs sometimes have long waiting lists.

Intelligence

Small dogs can excel at exercises that most small-dog owners would think of as impossible.

Dogs vary tremendously in their intelligence, just as humans do. It is quite difficult to determine a dog's actual intelligence, because so much depends on the way he has been brought up. Often very intelligent dogs have the misfortune of belonging to owners who don't understand dogs. These highly intelligent canines often gain the most unjustified description of stupid or naughty, when really it's just that they are misunderstood.

Dogs do not set out to be disobedient or naughty; they do

not have the capacity to be vindictive or cruel—these qualities are human, and we should do the dog justice by not attributing them to him also. He is merely an animal, reacting to the situation around and in front of him. He cannot look into the future to ponder on the consequences of his

The dog knows how to lie down but must be taught that our word 'down' is a signal for him to go into that position. He has no way of knowing unless we teach him.

actions, nor reflect on the past. It could be argued that a dog can think ahead, for how else can he know that at the end of a flyball set of hurdles, he catches the ball then races back over the hurdles to his handler, all with just one word of command at the start.

The way that the dog understands a series of actions initiated by a single command goes something like this: a command comes from the handler; with the stimulus of seeing a hurdle in front of him, his conditioned response, taught by the handler, is to jump over on the command, then over the next hurdle and so on until he gets to the flyball machine; he has been taught by his handler that when the machine is in front of him he must press it to gain his reward, which is the released ball; as the ball comes out, the dog's trained conditioned response is to catch it; with ball in mouth his conditioned response is to return to the handler, over the hurdles which he has been conditioned to jump when they appear in front of him. Each little stage acts as a catalyst to entice the dog to

Each obstacle which comes into the dog's vision is a trigger that sets off a brain reaction.

react to the next stage. He is conditioned and shaped by the handler to follow that certain routine. The whole thing is fun, which heightens the speed and enjoyment and leaves the dog eager for more (see also Triggers, Shaping).

Dogs are sensitive to human emotion and will react to the psychological climate around them. A calm handler will find it relatively easy to control an excitable dog, but a high-strung person will have much more difficulty as his own state of mind will excite the dog even more, often to such a point that the dog just cannot sit still and be calm at all. I usually suggest that such handlers take yoga lessons to learn how to control themselves before they can seriously learn how to control their dog.

It could be said that an intelligent dog will refuse to do certain things because he cannot see the purpose, or because it is easier to lie by the fire. Is this and intelligent dog? It's more likely that this is a dog who does not receive enough motivation from his handler. Dogs need to find an action rewarding in some small way at least. Maybe he just does not understand what you are talking about, due to insufficient training and shaping, or incorrect timing. Even if you are asking him to do some action that he has carried out before, it could be that the context is different in some way; and, in this particular situation, he does not understand that you mean the same thing.

The context does not have to be very different to you, but one small change can mean a world of difference to a dog. An example is teaching a dog to jump a small hurdle on the command 'jump.' If we take away that hurdle and say 'jump,' a human would know what is meant but a dog might be totally bewildered. So it is not unreasonable to think that, if you teach your dog to sit on the command 'sit' and do all your training on a mat or in the kitchen, when you take away the mat or change rooms the dog may well be bewildered, if he had associated your command with that mat or the kitchen surroundings. It may not even be as simple as the general surrounding, as he may have associated the command 'sit' with specific fact of being in front of a bucket in the kitchen. Simply take the bucket away, and he is not so sure. So you see it is not always just what you are doing that is shaping the dog but the environment as well, which is why it is important to change your place of training regularly to make sure that it's not external influences that are determining or influencing the dog's reaction (see also Training).

Facing page:
Border Collies are the biddable aids of the sheep farmer, and a peaceful house does not provide sufficient stimuli to satisfy this active and intelligent breed so outdoor exercise time is crucial.

Jealousy

I have two dogs amongst my 'pack' who spend most days in each other's company. One is a medium-sized long-coated crossbreed, the other is a very small Jack Russell Terrier, who is almost as small as a Chihuahua. Occasionally the small one displays what we as humans might term jealousy. If the larger dog is excited as I come into the room, or at feeding time, the little one jumps up and down grabbing at the larger dog's coat and tries to pull her away. She appears to all intents and purposes as if she is jealous. But dogs do not have such emotions. The little dog is merely excited by the situation, and my appearance heightens matters. If the little dog goes too far, the larger one snaps and reprimands her, and the situation calms down.

If the situation is likely to cause problems, for example, if the little dog retaliated to the snap and we ended up with a fight, I would have to intervene. The reason for the little dog's impertinence is the desire to get the best of whatever is on offer (see Dominance). But, of course, this action derives from the natural instinct of the need to survive (see Aggression over food).

Jumping Up

Many times I receive a desperate phone call from an owner whose dog jumps up at visitors. If only they had started correctly by insisting on control in the first place; but, I'm sure that we can all say, 'if only,' a few times in our lives. Anyone with the problem of the dog's jumping up will notice that it seems he only has muddy paws when the visitor is all dressed up in his Sunday best—a most infuriating situation, but one that, with a controlled training programme, can easily be sorted out.

It is too late to do something when a visitor arrives, so we must set up the situation with a friend. Get your dog under control, on a lead and collar, by your side in the sit position. Ask your friend to approach you. If the dog goes forward towards the person, snatch back with the lead with the action described in heelwork (as if you were saving him from touching a hot stove). Bring him back by your side; relax

Dogs and puppies jump up to gain close contact. They can be taught that love and affection are given when all four paws are firmly on the floor.

the lead and praise him in the sit position. Ask your friend to approach again. If the dog lunges forward, repeat the process by snatching back with the lead, relaxing and bringing him back into the sit, saying 'Oscar sit; good boy.' As your friend approaches again, the dog may start to realise—if your timing is correct—that it is more pleasurable to sit by your side on a loose lead. Next, allow your friend to approach, and stroke your dog, still keeping him in the sit position. If he tries to jump up, go back to the beginning and start again until he begins to understand what is required.

If your dog jumps up at you and you wish to stop it, there are a couple of methods you can use. First, face the dog as he approaches you. When you can see that he wants to jump up, raise your knee so that he hits his chest on your knee and cannot get the close contact that he desires. I might add that no force on your part is necessary or desirable, just a raised knee as a barrier. When he lands back on the floor, gently place him into the sit position and praise him. Thus

he starts to learn that praise and reward come when his feet are firmly on the floor.

Another method that works very well involves grabbing both front paws firmly in your hands as he jumps up. Hold them there and he will start to pull away, as he feels vulnerable when held up in this position. Let him struggle for a few seconds, then release him gently, praising him when he has all four feet firmly on the floor. Again, when it is repeated a few times, he will soon start to realise that it's much nicer to have contact with *terra-firma*.

I like to have close contact with my dogs and often choose to have them jump up. Obviously there are times when I don't want them to—for example, when I'm dressed up and ready to go out. So, I teach my dogs to jump up on a signal. I start when they are young, opening my arms and encouraging them to me. Their natural reaction is to jump up. I also teach them to stand back and not to jump by placing the flat of my hands in front of them as a barrier between us and giving a command of 'stay off.' If they try, they encounter my flat hands, and not the welcome of open arms and soon learn how to respond. Remember, if you do encourage your dog to jump up, then you must be very quick with your command to prevent it from happening when it is not practical or desirable.

Even though this Rottweiler is friendly, his sheer weight and power could knock someone over. If you want a dog like this one to jump up, you must teach him to do it only on command.

Kennels

At the mention of kennels most people think of boarding their dog whilst they go on holiday, but many people also choose to kennel their dogs at home.

Having a good secure kennel and run for your dog is a great idea if you are out for long periods, as the dog then has somewhere to relieve himself during the day, and you also avoid the problem of destructiveness caused by boredom in the house. Outside usually there is more to interest the dog, even if he's only watching the birds or listening to the wind in the trees. Kenneling at home can bring its own set of problems, such as excessive barking. Also, the dog can develop a distasteful doggy smell if he's kept in an area which is too small or not cleaned regularly. Sometimes dogs develop stereotypic behaviour if kenneled in a small area or if confined without sufficient outside stimuli. This behaviour shows itself in the form of compulsive circling or pacing up and down, or even sometimes the dog's throwing himself against the walls in an attempt to suppress the boredom. You may have seen this type of behaviour displayed in the old-fashioned type of zoos where wild animals were kept caged. These sorts of problems need not occur, however, if the dog is given sufficient exercise, space, and mental stimuli. These behaviours are the warning signs that things are not as they should be, and any such behaviour should be acted on straightaway by giving the dog a better quality of life and environmental enrichment. The ideal outdoor kennel is easily cleaned on a daily basis; the bedding should be freshened or washed at least twice a week. The kennel must be draft proof, weather proof, and large enough to provide a cool refuge in hot weather. A large well-fenced paddock area for the dog to run free is ideal—the larger it

Shown here is a nice small kennel and run courtesy of T. Ludberg.

is, the less likely you are to get the 'doggie' smell, as he will be able to urinate and defecate well away from his play and bed area. Of course, the dog will need a large container of water that he cannot tip. If you leave the dog with chews, bones, and/or toys, you must be certain that they cannot be injurious to the dog after constant chewing. I would rather be on the safe side and leave no more than a biscuit or two, until I return and can turn my full attention to his well-being.

BOARDING KENNELS

Boarding kennels are a necessity for most of us sometime in a dog's life, whether it is when we go on holiday or are too ill to look after him. Whatever the reason, it is as well to do your homework before hand. The standards differ tremendously from area to area. Any establishment that will not let you see the accommodations at any time during opening hours should be avoided like the plague—I shudder to think of what they might be hiding.

The basic minimum I would expect is that my dog have his own individual kennel and run, that there be facilities for free exercise in larger paddocks, and that there be no objection to keeping my dog on his normal diet. I would be very worried if the management did not point out that my dog must be fully inoculated, and I would look for an up-to-date kennel licence and insurance document, both of which should be clearly displayed on the wall of the reception area.

There are many excellent kennels, so have a look around your area and choose a good one well before you need it. If your dog has any special dietary or medical needs, let the proprietor know well in advance of your leaving the dog, so as to allow for all necessary arrangements.

As an owner of boarding kennels, and a frequent visitor to other people's, I can console you to the fact that dogs are not usually upset unduly by the experience. The well-adjusted and well-socialised dog accepts the experience happily and takes each day as it comes, making a great fuss of the kennel staff, often more than he does his owner. On occasion, more sensitive or timid dogs may be a little overwhelmed by the situation, but a good kennel will pay special attention to making his stay as comfortable as possible. Usually within one to two days, these dogs are quite relaxed.

Some dogs can be rather noisy in kennels, as the noise and presence of the other dogs excite them. Most kennel owners ignore the noise, and the dog soon learns that it has little effect. After a few days, most dogs settle into the kennel routine and calm down.

Much as it might boost our human ego to believe it, dogs do not sit wondering why you went off and left them, nor do they plot plans for their revenge upon your return. Their brain

Kennel floors must be of a sanitary, easy-to-clean, dry surface, such as concrete.

just doesn't work like that. Whilst he is in the kennel, your dog is thinking only about the situation going on around him, and he reacts to it. He is not thinking of the large marrow bone you might bring him back from the coast, even if you promised it before you left! He just cannot think like that.

Many dogs enjoy the life of kennels, and on a return visit will respond to the surroundings by pulling the owner in. You must not take this as an insult. The dog doesn't understand that you might be offended by his excitement on entering the kennels. All he understands is that the surroundings mean a pleasurable experience. So off you go and enjoy your holiday, in the certain knowledge that your dog will be happy and well cared for.

If you are unfortunate enough to inadvertently pick a kennel that sends your dog home dirty and unhappy, do not despair: write to or go to see the proprietor and tell him of your disappointment. It could be that he was unaware of the situation if he employs staff, and he will welcome your comments if he is a responsible kennel person. If you do not get any satisfaction, you can rest assured that word soon gets around if a place isn't up to scratch. Look around for good kennels that are run by people whom you can trust.

Teach the leave on command in a controlled situation with the dog on a lead. Once the dog understands, the command can be used in other situations.

Leave on Command

Dogs can be taught to leave and only touch when told to, but you must make sure that you are in a position to enforce the rules.

Leave on command is a most important command to teach your dog, as it could well prevent injury or danger. Your dog can be taught to leave things that he finds whilst out walking. Even in the cleanest of areas, objects can be found that could cause problems for your dog should he touch them, like mouldy chicken bones, a dead or injured animal, and all manner of strange items. So the command 'leave' and a watchful eye are most useful while out and about. Also, leave on command can be useful in the home, such as when the Sunday roast sits provocatively close to his nose, the baby drops her comforter, or the trash has tasty morsels.

I teach this command with a supply of my dog's favourite treats. I choose a calm quiet time with the dog by my side and on lead. I sit down, give him a titbit, and praise him. I then tell him to sit and carefully place a titbit on my knee. Keeping control with my lead, I say, 'leave,' and prevent the dog from getting the titbit. I use the checking action, as described in the walking to heel section, to prevent the dog from pulling towards the titbit. When he sits quietly for a few seconds, I pick up the titbit and give it to him. I repeat this process numerous times, and thus the dog learns that he must not touch unless told to do so. I then transfer this learning from the titbit to other items that he finds irresistible, such as slippers, children's toys, etc., giving a titbit or his own toy as reward. I train this command outside on a walk to prevent him from touching unsavoury items. When all training is completed, I then know that I have complete control of my dog in this respect, which is, of course, for his own good, as well as that of the family. Of course you must always be aware of what your dog is doing because, if you are not there to tell him not to touch, he may well investigate as his natural curious nature dictates.

Licking Faces

Commonly dogs lick the faces of children to get a taste of the sugary sweets left behind. Photo courtesy of B. Slater.

Have you ever wondered why dogs lick faces? If you consider the personalities of the dogs that do it, you are half way to the answer. It may be uncommon for a very dominant dog to lick your face, except maybe in a moment of submission. Puppies are the most frequent face lickers, and older, more submissive dogs do it quite frequently.

The action derives from the natural behaviour of puppies, who lick around the bitch's mouth to stimulate the regurgitation of food. It is a way of saying, in doggy terms, 'You're in charge; please feed me.'

Licking faces traces back to early puppyhood, and can be taken as a kind of submissive behaviour.

Obviously it is not a very hygienic habit to allow, particularly if you have children. The way to stop it from happening is simply to keep your face out of the way after a time of restricting the behaviour—just as a bitch would stand up out of the way of the older puppies.

Often older dogs lick small children's faces, which is more than likely because of the food that tends to be around a toddler's face. It is not a good idea to leave a dog with a child unattended at any time. But, in any case, you should try to feed your child out of reach of the dog, preferably by putting the dog outside so that the child cannot throw food to the dog, thus heightening the problem. Always make sure that your child's hands and face are free from food before he is allowed back in contact with the dog. Ensure that both dog and child learn the rules of living together safely.

Motivation

Most dogs will quite happily fit into our daily routines, once they understand the rules and become accustomed to our ways. They will go about their business taking each thing as it comes. Most difficulties arise when we want them to do something out of the ordinary, for example, fetch slippers, collect their own dish, or more complicated exercises such as ones necessary for competition work.

When you require something a little extra from your dog, motivation really comes into its own. The tasks that we want our dogs to perform seldom have good reason from a dog's eye view, and so we have to be ingenious and come up with ways to make the tasks seem more interesting and worthwhile.

Play training, reward training, shaping, timing and

A toy or treat can be used to help you become more interesting to your dog, and thereby make it easier for you to show him what is required and to gain successful results.

triggers are all concepts that you will find interesting when striving to motivate your dog. To carry out tasks that either he has already been taught, or is presently learning, the dog needs a little something that makes it all worthwhile. Just like us, he needs to feel that there is a reason to what he is doing. His reasons can be pretty basic, like food, reward by play, praise, or just love.

The more zest you want to see coming from your dog, the more motivation you must give him; and, therefore, more effort coupled with perfect timing must be given by you.

The dog can be likened to the user of a slot machine or one arm bandit. The user of these machines is kept interested by the now-and-again pay out. It does not pay out every time he puts in, nor does it pay in amounts equal to what he puts in, as it would pretty soon be boring. Rather, every so often it gives the player a bonus, at which point it has really got his attention. It then goes back to the little and often. The machines can be

addictive, and many people are regular players who come to know their machines intimately.

A dog can be likened to the player. If he were given a constant supply of prizes, however well meaning, he would pretty soon switch off and walk away. But when given excited bursts of reward or praise in return for correct actions, he gets really motivated and strives to get the right results. Occasionally he hits the jackpot and revels in the enjoyment, but to keep his attention we must then revert back to the lively outbursts when they are deserved. Sometimes small encouraging rewards are needed to keep up the momentum, and the best machines seem to know when they are needed: we must watch the reactions of our dog to learn when to give big pay outs and when small ones will suffice.

When you have learned how to motivate your dog, you have reached points that will put you well on the right track to being a good dog trainer.

Once the dog is motivated, there is not an end, by any means, that cannot be reached. Marcia Hoyt's Husky team traversing Alaskan terrain in the great Iditarod race.

Mouthing

Mouthing involves excessive grabbing of your hands or clothing. Your dog loves you. He wants to be with you. He wants you to play with him. He can't come up and tap you on the shoulder and say, 'Hey, want a game of tug?' So he uses his most effective means of communication, his mouth. If you have ever watched puppies playing, their mouths are used all the time for pulling and tugging at their pals. If the biting gets too hard, the other pup usually squeals and goes off to a corner to lick his wounds, refusing to play. In this way, pups learn a bite inhibition, i.e., they learn how hard they can bite before their friends say, 'I don't want to play with you any more; you hurt.'

Likewise with humans, if we imitate this behaviour, i.e., walk away and refuse to play when the going gets rough, the dog learns to play more gently. Have you ever wondered why dogs can be very gentle with children and quite rough with adults? We tend to look at it in human terms, but look from a dog's point of view: when the child suffers the slightest rough from the dog, that child runs away crying and refuses to play with the nasty puppy. When the child's curiosity and/or attraction takes over again, he again plays with the pup, so long as the pup doesn't get too rough. As soon as the pup gets too rough, the child goes away again. And so the pup learns very quickly that in order to play with the child, he must be gentle. Children are perfect passive dog trainers (see Passive Training).

Of course, I am not suggesting that you subject a child to an older dog who has not learnt to be gentle; but, by following this pattern and reacting in a hurt manner, you can train the dog yourself.

Remember there is no need to hit the dog or chastise him as this will only cause

Dogs communicate with their mouths. Keep your actions calm and quiet so as not to encourage biting. Refuse to play if your dog becomes too rough. He will soon learn that if he wants to play he must be gentle.

confusion—he may even think that it's part of the game, and then the matter becomes more intense. Simply act like a hurt child and withdraw your play, sit in a corner and whimper and lick your wounds, and the dog will very soon come over and apologise and will learn over a period of time to temper his bites to the gentle action that you can accept.

Neutering

Neutering basically involves the surgical removal of the dog's or bitch's sex glands. While it does involve anaesthesia, this surgery is relatively simple and has been successfully executed countless times. There are strong arguments in favour of neutering, yet the practice remains still a topic of debate for some fanciers.

MALE DOGS

If your dog is as you might say 'over-sexed,' e.g., he mounts people or tries to roam, looking for bitches, then castration may be the solution. It is not the foolproof way to solve the problem, but, in my estimation, it stands about an 80-percent chance of helping, providing you don't wait until the behaviour becomes habitual. Sometimes castration can help reduce dominant behaviour or aggression. The vet may be able to administer

drugs that mimic the effect of castration, thereby allowing you to see to some extent, at least, what the result of the operation might be, before having the irrevocable surgery performed. If you have no intention of breeding, then castration is certainly a good idea, as it reduces the likelihood of dominance problems and eliminates the possibilities of fathering unwanted puppies.

BITCHES

I firmly believe that all bitches who are bought as pets, without any intention of breeding, should be spayed, as soon as the vet allows. It is now generally regarded as an old-wives tale that it is better for the bitch to have a litter before she is spayed. There are already far too many unwanted puppies in the world—just ask any rescue centre—to breed merely for the sake of producing some more. One should think very carefully, especially if your dog is a crossbreed and not a true purebred, before stepping into the world of breeding, even if you intend to have only one litter. As a breeder you will have many moral and legal obligations. If you just want a pet, then have your bitch spayed and save yourself a lot of problems. If you really do want to breed, turn to my section on breeding where I deal with some of the many problems involved.

Some people report weight gain in their bitches after having them spayed, but it does not have to be a problem (see Obesity). The reason spayed bitches put on weight is because, without the urge to reproduce, they become less active sexually and otherwise. To keep them trim you must ensure that they get regular daily exercise together with a balanced diet. It is not necessary for them to put on weight if you keep them active.

It is not easy to produce such beautiful puppies as these Old English Sheepdogs—indeed, breeding should be left to the experts. Photo by L. Lopina for breeder-owners D. and J. Bankoviskis.

Obesity ———————

The more kind-hearted the person, the more difficult he seems to find it to control obesity in his dog.

A normal healthy dog who is fed a well-balanced diet and has plenty of regular exercise (even if neutered) should not become fat.

Let me start at the beginning with puppies. Young pups, like all other dogs, should have a good even covering of flesh but should not be overweight. Even if you think that it could be labelled 'puppy fat,' a fat puppy is putting excessive strain on his limbs that can lead to problems later (and sometimes sooner rather than later) in life. Fat puppies often become fat young adults—even if they run off the fat in adolescence, they often revert back to being fat adults later on. Just like humans, all dogs have varying metabolic rates, but we should not use this fact as an excuse.

It is commonly thought that spayed bitches automatically gain weight. Well, some do, but the reasons are not always so straightforward as the statement. A spayed bitch is no longer sexually active, which in itself can cause weight gain— 'active' being the operative word rather than 'sexually.' Because a spayed bitch no longer has the urge to find a mate, copulate, prepare a nest, etc., you will find that, unless you keep her fit with plenty of games, training, and exercise, she may well not be as active as before, and less active individuals are more prone to weight gain.

As dogs get older, they can also start to slow down and thus do not require the same amount of food as they did in their more active youth. As owners we often do not notice until the pounds start to creep on. Good frequent exercise, coupled with training and a good balanced diet must be a regular part of any dog's day.

As they say in all the best slimming clubs, 'Beware of sugary sweets and biscuits.'

Even spayed bitches, like this one, can remain fit and trim. By keeping your dog healthy, you help to avoid problems later in the dog's life.

Some dog biscuits may not appear to us to be sugary but may well have a very high sugar content. Read the ingredients carefully and stick to wholemeal biscuits, and only a bare minimum of these. If your dog is overweight, the first thing you should do is cut out all of those sugary or fatty treats, and only feed a set meal. If you want to use treats as part of your reward training, then be careful that the intake is taken from the dog's daily allowance. It's a good idea to prepare your dog's total intake for the day, as then you cannot be tempted to offer him an extra handful here and there. If your dog is seriously overweight, you should consult your vet who may recommend low-calorie food. But you must remember that food is not the only criteria, exercise plays a very important role, too (see also Feeding).

Old Age

As our faithful pets mature, they usually reach the stage where they seem to fit into our lives like a comfortable old shoe. They know all of the idiosyncrasies of our character and have learnt how best to get on with being our partners.

Often when a person gets a new puppy after loosing an old dog, he feels bitter and frustrated because the young dog does not fit in so beautifully. What that person forgets is that the old dog had probably 15 or more years to learn how to fit in. If the puppy does not jell within 15 weeks, we get worried. I hope that you are reading this section because your dog is advancing in years, and you will remember these words when the sad time comes and you have to replace him.

Old dogs, like old friends, always seem to know how you feel. They comfort you and take pleasure in your company. Young dogs, like new friends, can be lively, excitable, and perhaps not always have your interests at the top of their list of priorities.

Old dogs grow a little more independent because they have learnt the ground rules that have become the normal way of day-to-day life. They do not need to keep coming to you for reassurance that all is OK, like a young dog must. Old dogs do develop problems, and life is not always such smooth sailing. My oldest dog is stone deaf. She does not hear a thing, not even the postman! If she is asleep and we need to move her, she almost jumps out of her skin when we wake her, no matter how gently we try to do it. She is still as obedient as the day she won her first competition because she understands all the basic commands, which we have transferred into hand signals and gestures instead of words. As long as she is looking at us, she will instantly obey. It can be a problem if she is going in the wrong direction away from us, for then we have to race up to her (thank goodness she doesn't run so fast anymore) and tap her on the shoulder. She invariably is startled, as she has no idea that we are there; but, as soon as she sees our commands, she obeys with a happy and contented look on her face—I just hope that she doesn't go blind.

Other problems can develop, like blindness, incontinence, heart flutters, etc. You should always take veterinary advice for any of these problems, but most of them can be tolerated and/or treated to extend your partnership as long as humanly possible.

Sometimes there comes a time when life becomes very difficult to bear for an old dog, because of illness or infirmity. Your vet may well then suggest that the kindest way out is euthanasia, quietly and painlessly ending your dog's suffering. It is a most painful and upsetting decision to make, but sometimes it is the kindest. After a lifetime of happiness from your pal, it would be cruel to let him end his days in

We grow so close to our canine companions that it is hard to imagine our life without them.

suffering.

Animals do not understand the concept of death and will trust you until the end. So, if the dreaded time comes, do not prolong the dog's agony by misguided self pity, but do whatever is best for the dog.

Passive Training—

No, it's not a new fangled training method: it's what we all do every day with our dogs without realising that we are doing it; it's the conditioning of occurrences in day-to-day life; it's the reactions to situations as they occur; it's things that we don't perceive though they are happening all the time; it's the things that are put in the dog's way that prevent him from reacting in certain ways; and it's the things that almost shout out, 'Go ahead,' but are just a part of daily life. We should think carefully about these things when our dog's behaviour has to be altered or shaped in some way.

Passive training involves tapping into the reasons behind the reactions, the things that we think we have never taught our dogs and yet they somehow know. We may change some small thing in the house that may be the trigger that sets off a chain of reactions in your dog (see Triggers).

Don't be afraid to watch carefully your dog's reactions, and analyse what is happening at the same time. What are you doing? What time of day is it? And even, what is the TV showing? The very act of your walking from the lounge to the kitchen may trigger a reaction in your dog. For example, he may rush to the kitchen and scavenge in the bin (see Thieving). You've never taught the dog to do it consciously, but, it happened once and the dog gained great pleasure from a tasty morsel therein; so, without going anywhere near the dog, you trained him to do something without even realising it.

Some of these behaviour patterns are the strongest and most difficult or time consuming to beat, because it takes us mere humans so long to realise that something was happening and that the dog was learning from it.

A few years ago a lady

If you let your dog in because he jumps on the door, you may be passively training him to jump up. Photo courtesy of owner L. Abraham.

phoned in desperation. She had a springer spaniel who at 18 months old had taken to defecating up the kitchen walls and doors, necessitating newspapers to be stuck over the doors and walls to protect them. The solution to this dilemma is explained in the section on housetraining. The crux of the problem was caused by the owners' gradually increasing the area that they covered with the newspaper (just in case!), and the springer, being well trained, happily obliging by performing wherever the paper was stuck— a perfect example of passive training, or training an act without realising it and, indeed, whilst trying to achieve the exact opposite.

To further understand passive training, we can look at those dogs who just 'know' when it's walkies time or home-from-work time for dad. Dogs know such times not because they are psychic but because they have been passively trained. Dogs do have an inbuilt body clock, which, like ours, reacts to daylight, length of day, and other factors. To know when something is about to happen is not caused by psychic phenomenon but by passive training: it could be something as remote as a distant train going by just before dad arrives home each day (something which you wouldn't notice yourself but which the dog picks up on) or it could be something nearer to home like the kettle being switched on or the end of a given television show. Dogs take in far more than we do in part because their world is far less complicated. They better tune in to their surroundings because they don't have thoughts going through their

heads like what to prepare when the Joneses are coming to dinner, or whether Susan will get good grades at school. They do not have that capacity. They only know if the situation that they are experiencing now is pleasurable or unpleasurable. If it is pleasurable they react to that particular trigger (see Triggers), and, if everything is as it normally is, they react in anticipation of the pleasurable thing that is about to happen, triggered by the action or circumstances beforehand.

We can passively teach the exact opposite to what we are trying to achieve by inadvertently ignoring or not noticing the dog's reactions to our actions. For instance, in teaching a dog to walk to heel (or so we think), we can systematically teach the dog to pull, if we are pre-occupied by our thoughts or surroundings and just go through the motions, not watching the dog's reactions, and check him back saying, 'Heel, good dog,' after which the dog surges forward again. The timing is wrong (see Timing), and is coupled with a monotonous drone (see

Motivation); and, all in all, the dog both ignores and disregards the training attempts. It means nothing. In fact, because the dog is allowed to pull, the pressure 'round his neck actually gives him a form of relief (see Unusual Behaviour), and he learns that to pull is the normal policy. For you, the owner, it is passive training in that you don't realise that you are doing it; but, for the dog, it is quite positive training of the pull reaction.

Teaching the dog to sit is typically an easy task; but, if a dog has been passively trained to reject the sit position, training can be made very difficult.

Dogs can play with an almost obsessive intensity. Photo courtesy of owner L. Abraham.

Playing ———————

Playing is a natural part of development. It helps pups to realise their station in life. They practice through play all the roles that they might have to take later in life, from aggressor to lover. It is a necessary part of growing up, and those deprived of play often show behavioral problems later on.

Play and training should go together to create a happy well-adjusted pet (see Play Training). You must remember that a puppy cannot turn into an adult overnight—he must be allowed to play.

Dogs play various games such as tugging, chewing, chasing and mock killing. Controlling these play sessions with your dog will make control later in life far easier. Toys should always remain your property (see Toys), and the dog should not be allowed to guard or possess them. Many owners make the mistake of allowing their dog to collect all the toys together and keep them with him. This hoarding should be discouraged as it can readily lead to protective aggression.

Once I have a puppy playing with a toy, I like to put him on a light lead so that I can gently reel him in and take the toy as part of the game, and thus I remain in control the whole time. This activity can be developed into a game of fetch later on (see Retrieve). The choice of toys for your pet is varied (see Toys), but make sure that what you choose is safe for the dog, and make certain that the toy remains your property and not the dog's.

There is probably no more pleasurable way to train than through play training—both you and your dog can derive great enjoyment from it.

Play Training

In my view, the best way to train a dog is through play. Children learn through play, and it is known that children can develop all sorts of extreme compulsive and un-natural behaviour patterns in cases where they are deprived of play. Play training helps tremendously with motivation to give the dog that want-to-please and work-for-you mentality.

DOGS WHO WON'T PLAY

Dogs often seem to lack the knowledge of how to play because of the way they have been raised, particularly if it is coupled with a placid canine temperament. But, while it may take some time, just about every dog can be taught to play—they can be motivated into enjoying a game with you.

If your dog lacks enthusiasm for play, then try the following training programme. First, remove all toys, balls, chews, and other such objects from the

A young boy's interest in his dog, coupled with the child's natural exuberance for play, can often motivate any dog to play.

reach of your dog. Observe your dog's behaviour pattern for a few days and watch for moments of exuberance, which may be difficult to detect in some dogs, so watch carefully for them. During this time, don't make a fuss of him. Basically ignore him and his demands, except of course for his feeding, watering and basic bodily needs. In essence, pretend that he doesn't exist for a day or two. I know that it might seem hard, but it's worth it in the long run.

When you have established a relatively consistent time when he is at his most exuberant, e.g., before feeding or walking, take a tug toy and start playing with it yourself. Do not at this stage invite the dog to join you, but just play by yourself with the toy. If the dog tries to join you, great, but allow him to do so for a few moments only, and then put away the toy. At all other times ignore the dog. Follow this sequence as many times a day as you have detected excitement. Don't try to get the dog to join in, but allow him to do so if he shows an interest. This procedure works particularly well when the dog is hungry, as it heightens his excitement. Always remember to put the toy away, out of the dog's reach. He must only be allowed to play when he plays with you. Ignore the dog the rest of the time.

Once the dog has shown some interest and shown a desire to join you (and this can take a while with older or more blasé dogs), the toy can then be left in sight, yet still out of reach. Leaving the toy in sight heightens the anticipation of play as the dog can see the toy but not get to it until you arrive to have a game. Gradually the dog will want to play; but, this method only works if you refrain from pushing the dog into play—let him acquire the 'want' on his own. Continue keeping other contact to a minimum until you are confident that your dog will play on the production of his toy. The procedure can be repeated to wean the dog onto other toys, although it shouldn't take as long the second or third time around.

You can start to incorporate the playing into training, but use very short sessions at the start. This method also works exceptionally well with dogs who are possessive over their toys or will play only with the toy but not with you.

Do not loose faith. As I say, it can take a while, but it does work.

Time out for play is a great way to keep the dog motivated.

HOW TO USE IT

The toy can be used in all sorts of ways during training to aid motivation (see Motivation). It can be used as an immediate reward for carrying out a task or as an inducement to react to your command. It can be used as an incentive to heighten enthusiasm, and introduced at any time during an exercise to enliven the dog. It can also be used to distract the dog from things that you don't want him to do. Do not over-use the toy at the start. If your dog has not been a good player in the past, you don't want to bore him or you'll end up back at square one (see Motivation). Likewise, with an over-excitable dog, too much of the toy will prevent him from concentrating on the task ahead. Watch your dog and

The Nylafloss has proven a favourite of many dogs and can be an excellent device for motivating the dog.

learn from his reactions. Don't be afraid to watch a training exercise go wrong, because by observing carefully you are able to put things right much more quickly and efficiently—and without distress and confusion being loaded on to the dog. It is far better to isolate a problem by watching and reacting correctly than to use a hit-and-miss approach.

Many dogs are happy to play with the handler alone and do not need a toy to motivate them. When I get a new puppy, I always aim to teach the dog to play with me—to have a rough and tumble, to chase after my fingers, and to play tug of war with a handkerchief or something that will always be there. Thus, I always have my motivational tools to hand. They never run out, get lost, or disappear, which puts me at a great advantage in times when quick reactions are needed, e.g., when I need the dog to come to me quickly while out walking, or in the competition ring where no toys are allowed.

Training through play is the most satisfactory and pleasurable way of training. It brings pleasure to the dog, to the handler, and to all who witness it (see also Toys, Reward Training, Distraction Training, Motivation).

Pulling

Owners find dogs who have learnt to pull quite difficult to re-train, because inadvertently they have already taught them to pull, often systematically over a period of weeks, months, and sometimes years (see Passive Training). Whatever command you have used to train your dog to heel (or rather not to heel), you should decide upon another command to coincide with your new approach to training. If you have already 'trained' your dog to pull on the lead to the command of 'heel', then use something else such as 'close.' Before you proceed, I strongly recommend that you read the section on timing.

The object now is to teach the dog that it is pleasant to be by your side and boring or uncomfortable to be at the end of the lead, or to be pulling.

Choose a collar which fits your dog comfortably and is not too long if it has a checking action. Also choose a nice soft lead which is comfortable to

your hands.

Choose a quiet place to start your training, away from other dogs, people, and distractions so that you and your dog can concentrate. Bring your dog into a sit by your side. Make sure that his collar is comfortable and sitting fairly high around his neck, which is particularly important with the heavy, stronger dogs.

Get your dog's attention by talking excitedly and playfully to him, or by showing him his toy. Then step off remembering that it must be a pleasant experience to be with you. Every time your dog looks at you he must see pleasure or reward. The moment your dog starts to pull to the end of your lead, you should immediately check him back with a snatch as if you were saving him from something hot. You will probably need to reach forward with the lead to give yourself some slack before snatching back; and, as the dog comes toward you he should see a pleasant smiling face and the reward of his toy or your voice and hands telling him how clever he is, coupled with his new heel command (let's say 'close,') As he comes back towards you, all he gets is pleasure. If he goes away from that heel position, it is uncomfortable. So where is the best place to be? Sounds easy, doesn't it? But the all-important part is timing. A split second of incorrect timing and the dog becomes most confused and frustrated and 'switches off.' Repeat the process, but never allow the lead to go tight. If he starts to go ahead, reach forward with the lead and check him back into the correct position—no harsh words, only pleasure and comfort beside you.

You will find it beneficial to read the section on walking to heel. Quite often this simple conditioning is all it takes. If you can restrict yourself from taking the dog out on a lead and allowing him to pull whilst the re-training programme takes place, then the puppy-training method will work for

you, too.

Whichever method you choose, the abundant pleasure must always be derived from the dog's being in the correct position. Never chastise your dog when he *is* in the correct position, however long it took you to get him there. The first time that you do it, you take your training backwards by weeks.

Once you can get your dog to walk to heel in a quiet place, you can then introduce a few distractions. When perfection is found again, you can go on to busier places until your dog is confident and happy to stay by your side in all situations.

The most pleasurable time that I experienced when I really appreciated my dog's enjoying walking to heel was not as you might expect in a contest but at the seaside when I was able to tuck the lead in my pocket and walk along the promenade eating the great British tradition, fish and chips, with a dog that did not pull my hand away from my mouth and without fear of losing my dinner!

Punishment

In days of old, most dog trainers were of the opinion that to be in charge of the dog you needed to rule with the rod, i.e., use physical punishment to chastise. Today, thank goodness, things have changed, and it is recognised that kindness, guidance and praise for correct behaviour are far more beneficial, and reap much better results. In my view, dogs, somewhat more basic than humans and lacking the power of lateral thinking, respond even better than children do to rearing in accordance with this philosophy.

I, like most other dog trainers of my era, started at a time when it was more important to learn a method of teaching an exercise than to understand what made a dog tick. Most methods were derived from the police-dog-training techniques just after the First World War, and a 'lick them into shape by fair means or foul' sort of attitude

prevailed.

Thank goodness that most trainers, like me, have realised that there is far more to dogs than meets the eye, and consequently the degree of excellence in training seems to get ever higher. Punishment, any more than a raised tone of voice or a quick shake, is rarely, if ever, necessary. A well-reared dog will never need to, or even know how to, misbehave, and therefore anything that goes wrong is due to misunderstanding, lack of training, or natural instinct—none of which should be blamed on the dog.

Obviously our dogs will sometimes choose a different reaction to a situation to the one that we might have chosen, but a simple word of command like 'No' to prevent the action, followed by guidance to show the dog what is the correct reaction, will soon put things right. We must remember that our dogs are only animals and

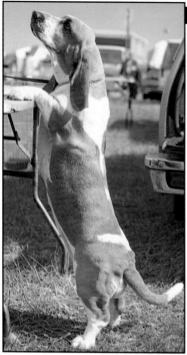

Proper training is far better than punishment for shaping a dog's behaviour. If the dog has behaved incorrectly, punishment often serves only to confuse matters. Photo of Basset Hound by I. Francais.

just sit back and watch problems develop and then chastise, because once the dog has done something incorrectly the very action of doing it has been implanted in his brain as a possible reaction to that situation. The more times something goes wrong, the more chances that the same error will be repeated in the future, because that reaction is difficult to erase, especially if it is followed by a very positive reward or relief. The way in which the dog's brain works means that sometimes chastising an action can only cause the dog to react in the same manner next time, but he tries to do it quicker in order to avoid the end part, namely the punishment. So it's better to prevent misconduct and guide dogs into good or more desirable behaviour.

Punishment rarely works to solve the problem that you are punishing; but, it certainly does enforce in the dog that you are not to be trusted. To learn how to correct your dog's actions without punishment, see the sections on distraction training, reward training, timing, and shaping.

cannot read our minds.

I usually use the call-away method when any of my dogs start to stray from my standards. If they are about to do something wrong, I simply call them to me and show them the right way to behave. I don't

Recall

The recall, or 'coming back,' is one of the most important exercises to teach if you want your dog to be part of the family, to go on outings with you, and run free, safe in the knowledge that he will come back when called, every time, without question. If you intend to let your dog loose in public areas, you must be absolutely positive that he will come bounding back the second you call him, whatever the distractions. If he doesn't, I'm sure that you do not need me to tell you what problems might occur.

An extending lead can give you control at a distance in the stages between on-lead and off-lead recalls.

With very young puppies, recall is easy. The safest, most comfortable place to be for a tiny pup who is let out in the big wide world is with mum (or dad)!

Even before he has completed his inoculations, you can be starting the basics of the recall in the garden and other safe places. Simply walk along with the dog on lead, and then quite suddenly back off, giving a little playful jerk on the lead; at the same time, call the dog's name and the command 'come.' Reel him in with lots of fuss and play to make it exciting for him to be with you. Use your voice in differing light tones to be welcoming, and use your hands to give affection and security. Never ever chastise your dog for coming to you, however frustrated you may feel at the situation.

When your dog is playing in the garden or the house, frequently call him to you. Use anything you can to ensure that he wants to come when he is called: food, toys, titbits, biscuits or just love. Whatever you use, 'make sure that you are in a position to make him want to come to you instantly.

Once out in the big wide world, begin on the lead and proceed as before. Walk a little way, then back off calling his name and giving the command 'Oscar come,' lots of praise, and love. Next find a nice quiet place in the middle of an open field so that you can be fully aware of any strangers or loose dogs approaching. Sit down on the grass, let your dog loose, and play with him. Take with you a favourite toy, and have a good game, calling him frequently using the command 'come' together with his name and lots of fuss. We are now starting to build up a conditional idea in the dog's mind that the nicest place in the world to be is with you. The word 'come' means pleasure, fuss, love, or a game. Brought up in this way, why should any dog not want to be with you?

You can progress with these little games, so that you have a short walk and then another game. The dog must learn that coming back to you means fun. Do not just let him loose and then call him back when you want to go home. Call him frequently, play, and make a fuss.

I like to have a special toy to produce from my pocket just for these games. I do not let the dog have the toy—it's mine—but he can play with me and the toy when he comes to me. I don't allow him to run off with the toy, for then I wouldn't have the toy for him to come to. But when he comes, we have a really good game. The toy is the kind that we can both hold at the same time. I use a piece of thick knotted rope called Nylafloss®. It has tasseled ends, and my dogs love it. But whatever toy you choose, the important factors are that the toy belongs to you and not the dog, that he is not to be allowed the toy unless he is actively playing with you, and that the

Have a game with your dog to let him know that to come on your command is far more fun than anything elsewhere.

toy be put away out of reach when you are not playing together (see Toys).

Don't follow these instructions parrot fashion, as there is nothing more likely to make your dog look elsewhere for his recreation than a droning, boring voice, even if it is saying, 'Good boy.' Be lively, be interesting, be fun for him. Be his friend and companion, not just the boss (see also Motivation).

Many people let their dogs off lead before they have taught them what 'come' means. After one-half-hour's chase and a sore throat from yelling, the dog finally comes back usually because he's grown bored with his surroundings. What does he get? 'You stupid dog, where have you been? I'm late for the office!' and lots of other verbal aggression. (Unfortunately, sometimes people hit the dog, too.)

Well, would *you* come back next time? I know what I would do, I'd put as much space as I could between my owner and myself and keep it there as long as I dare!

If you get yourself into this unfortunate position, remember that you must be pleasant and fun. When he eventually comes back, spend a few moments having a game—you're late anyway, so a few more moments won't hurt, and you stand a much better chance of getting him back next time if you are nice.

Another frustrating problem occurs when your dog comes back to you, but then runs away as soon as you go to connect the lead. This is quite a common problem. The dog thinks that it's all one big game and derives great fun from darting away encouraging you into a chase. If you look at the posture of a dog when he is inviting play, his front end goes down and his back end up in the air. Compare this to the posture you go into when you lean forward to attach the lead. The instant down is one effective way to solve this dilemma.

THE INSTANT DOWN

The instant down is a no-fuss way of getting your dog to where you want him, and often is the answer for people whose dogs have already learnt that they can do as they please

Giving your dog a reward for coming on command helps to convince him to obey in the future. If, on the contrary, you chastise him, he is likely to think twice the next time. Photo by I. Francais of Border Collie owned by Vivian Bregman.

when off lead. After you have already taught your dog the meaning of the down command, this extension of the exercise can be taught. The training should follow two parallel routines.

METHOD 1.) Walk with your dog on the lead and then, without warning the dog, turn quickly and put him into the down position, giving a firm command of 'Down.' Don't just command him, but physically put him in the down. Keep him there for a few seconds and then release him and walk on. Repeat this a few times at each session.

METHOD 2.) Play with your dog and his favourite toy, keeping him on the lead. When you have his full attention, shorten the lead and physically

Teaching the 'instant down' is important because it may one day save your dog's life.

put him into the down. Giving the command 'Down,' give him his toy as reward. The object of the exercise is to get him down as fast as possible, as if his life depended on it. One day you may be glad that you taught him this exercise as his life could well depend on it in an emergency.

Extend these training routines to outside, and, of course, teach them fully on the lead before you ever take him off lead. If your reactions are quick and your timing is right (see Timing), your dog will start to drop on command, of his own accord—and will, in fact, beat you to it. Remember to practice regularly if you want your dog's reactions to your commands to remain constant and instant.

This instant down can then be used if your dog won't come back or 'goes deaf.' It gets better results than the recall as it is a much more positive and definite command. Once the dog is in the 'down', you have his full attention, and you can then either go over to him and attach his lead, or call him to you now that he is controlled. It's a good idea to do the instant down three or four times whilst you are out even if you don't need it, as this will keep his reactions sharp.

Always have a game with him afterwards, so that he doesn't come to associate the down with a negative, boring exercise.

If your dog tends to ignore you at a distance or when other dogs or children are around, then it is a good idea to use the training method with which we started. Attach a long line so that the dog can experience relative freedom but has no

In the early stages of training, you may wish to give a treat when the dog is in the down to help reinforce the desired behaviour.

The recall exercise should be pleasurable and fun. This dog is obviously frightened and apprehensive, and the handler must skilfully overcome the dog's fears.

option but to come when called as you reel him in on the line. Let him roam around awhile, then call him and give a little jerk on the line when he's not looking. Praise him and reel him in, in a happy excitable manner. Have a game and then let him 'do his own thing' again. Repeat this numerous times, and over the course of a few weeks he will learn that it's good fun to come when called.

Once you have taught your dog to sit or down and stay confidently, you can bring in a more formal type of recall. As you may have seen at dog clubs or obedience shows, the dog is left in the sit or down position, whilst the handler walks away a short distance and then turns and calls the dog to him.

Eventually the dog can be taught to come and sit in front of you. However, start with just calling him and making lots of fuss. The most important thing is that he wants to come, and his attention is kept on you. If you get too formal too soon, he will get bored, and he won't feel such a thrill in coming to you. The start of the formal exercise is, of course, done on the lead. You need the lead as an extension to your arm to give the dog confidence and to help him understand.

So keep it light, keep it fun, be a team with your dog, and enjoy it. But remember that dogs won't come to aggressive, boring, dull, uninteresting handlers. Would you?

Retrieving

Most puppies and young dogs enjoy carrying around toys, balls, or sticks that they find while out walking, and owners take great delight in extending this natural reaction into a game of throw and retrieve. Before I go any further, I should like to point out about the danger of throwing sticks. If a stick is thrown for your dog and its end lands in the ground, it is quite possible that your vet will make an unfortunate fee from removing the stick after the dog has landed on it, and it has gone through the dog's palate. This happens very often, but owners never seem to think it will happen to them. In fact I know one young boy whose dog died following such an unfortunate occurrence. So I always take with me on walks a ball or toy for my dogs to retrieve.

If your dog will carry a toy, it is a simple extension to teach him the game of fetch. While he is happy in the house with his toy, slip on his lead so that you have control. Tease him with the toy and then throw it a short distance. Allow him to go and pick it up, incorporating the command 'fetch' or 'hold.' Then call him and gently reel him in on the lead, praising him all the time. If he drops his toy, stop the praise, pick up the toy, and start again. Don't chastise him, as this will only confuse him. Remember that the praise and encouragement come only when he is holding his toy and not if he drops it. Likewise, once he has delivered the toy to you, don't go overboard on the praise, as this will teach him to drop it before he gets to you: he will think the praise comes for the drop.

This method can be extended in distance, but keep the lead on until you are certain that your dog will come back each time. Don't give him the option of thinking that fetch means 'do what you like,' and you will have many happy hours while out walking, playing as a team.

If your dog does not carry toys around naturally, or if you wish, go on to competition work where your dog can be taught to retrieve more formally. Some breeds take a little longer than others, but proper retrieving, more than any other basic exercise, depends on perfect timing.

The one important underlying factor to remember is that the dog must be praised at the very time he is doing the correct action and not after. Of course, it sounds like common sense, but you will be surprised by how easy it is to fall into the latter trap.

I will explain each step:

Choose an article that is easy for the dog to hold and soft on his mouth. Have a little game with the dog, keeping him on the lead, but getting him in an attentive frame of mind. Then calmly guide him to your side. Place him in the sit, gently open his mouth, and pop in the article saying, 'Hold, good boy.' Take the article within seconds so that he has no chance to spit it out. He may well try to stand up, struggle, and reject the article, but keep calm and friendly. Don't get annoyed, as he will only get

If your dog does not naturally retrieve, he can be taught by gentle repetition and precise timing with praise— timing is of paramount importance.

confused and may connect your annoyance with the article. He will then try all the harder to reject it next time. The more you get annoyed, the more he fights it, and you end by giving up in desperation.

Half a second of the article in his mouth, coupled with pleasure and praise, will lead to a full second tomorrow, and so on, step by step, until he understands what 'hold' means. If your timing is excellent, you will see favorable results very quickly. If you have tried before with a forceful method or incorrect timing, you will have to take things very slowly, gaining the dog's confidence as you go.

Pleasure is the key word: keep it happy and don't lose your temper. Half a second of getting it right is worth far more than a five-minute struggle. Practice your timing without the dog. Pretend your left hand is the dog's mouth. Say 'Hold' and place the article, open your hand, take out the article, and be quiet. The praise must come while the article is in the dog's mouth and not when it has been given up. They who get the timing right to

Golden Retrievers demonstrate their instinct to retrieve at an early age, as evidenced in this young pup.

start with often lose it as soon as they see success—they are so delighted that the dog has held and then given up the article that they go overboard on the praise when the dog has completed the action. The dog responds quickly to the praise, and before you know it, he's spitting it out before you go to take it in anticipation of his praise. Then back to square one!

You will pretty soon see that the dog is taking an interest, and will start to reach out for the article of his own accord. To extend the exercise, allow him to reach out and take the article using your command and praise, and then guide him back towards you whilst he is holding the article, using your lead to gently reel him in. In this way, he learns to go out, pick up, and bring back. You can gradually extend the distance and lower the article nearer to the floor, keeping your hand on the article at first to give him confidence. As your success grows, don't be tempted to go too fast, i.e., don't take him off lead and throw the

If you take your time, be kind and patient with your dog, then you will be rewarded.

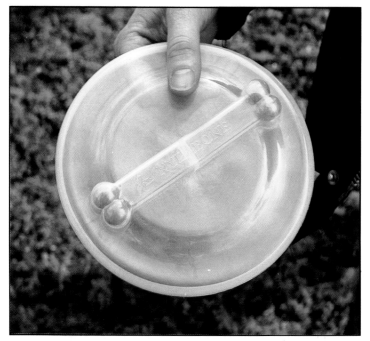

The Gumadisc® for dogs is a soft, flexible disc that is very safe and durable. The bone on top makes it easy to retrieve.

article a long distance, because he may not necessarily connect this new action with the old one. The distance must be built up very gradually.

If you are interested in competition work, then the retrieve, as all other basic exercises, will need more precision. This method gives you a perfect start, and your dog will be happy and confident to retrieve.

Reward Training—

Rewards can come to a dog in very many guises. Once there is a good rapport between you and your dog, he can detect very subtle movements and gestures that say to him you are pleased (or not), often without your even being aware of your communication. You will find that when you are particularly pleased with your dog, he will be over keen to be close to you and drink in your pleasure.

Most people will find it easier and more positive to reward the dog by use of a happy light voice, a titbit, or a friendly pat. This is quite sufficient for most dogs to know that what they are doing brings the approval of their human friend. You notice that I say 'what the dog *is* doing,' which is the all-important factor in giving rewards of any kind in return for good or acceptable behaviour. The dog cannot think back to what he *was* doing a moment ago. In his

eyes the reward comes for what he is doing **now**, at the very moment the reward is given. So, if I am teaching Oscar to lie down, I give him the down command and also the actions that show him what the word means. Whilst he is down, I give him his reward, ensuring that he stays down. Thus he receives the reward for staying down when told. If I waited until he got up, no matter how much I told him he was good for staying down, in his eyes all the reward and praise came as soon as he got up, so he quickly starts to associate 'down' with jump up and get a reward! You can see how easy it is to confuse him. He cannot for the life of him imagine why you are displeased. He thinks that he has done as requested, and he has, but it is not what you thought you were requesting!

Dogs do not understand language. They can only learn an action in connection with a certain sound (word). The only meaning that word or sound has to the dog is the one that he interprets from our actions. So, if our timing is slightly out, the word or sound that we are trying to get him to connect with an action can be interpreted by the dog as something completely different.

Remember that rewards and praise, like correction of undesirable acts, must come simultaneously with the action, not before or even fractionally after.

As I said at the start of this

Use rewards thoughtfully in conjunction with your training, and your dog has an added incentive to respond to you.

section, gentle praise from the handler is reward enough for many dogs. If you like to give a titbit, that's fine, but be careful that you do not upset your dog's digestive system—some dogs cannot tolerate colourants, sugars, and other additives found in some treats (see Diet, Treats).

For most dogs, there is nothing more rewarding than gentle praise and a kind hand. Photo by R. Reagan of Mastiff owned by Winterwood Kennels.

The only foolproof way to prevent roaming is a well-fenced garden from which your dog cannot escape.

Roaming

Often I get calls from owners who say that their dogs keep getting out and roaming. These dogs are a nuisance to others, and, of course, may cause a road accident.

Once a dog has been allowed (by accident or design) to wander on his own, this action will be catalogued in his brain, normally as a pleasurable pursuit, and he will take every opportunity to repeat this pleasing experience.

It takes a great deal of training to teach a dog that it should not go over a given boundary, more training than most people are willing to provide. Even with highly trained dogs, I would not be 100% sure that, given certain circumstances, they would not cross a set boundary.

The only foolproof method is to ensure that your garden or yard is fully secure, or to put your dog on to a retractable tether line. Fencing can be expensive, but a tether or line is relatively inexpensive in comparison to the pain and suffering you might cause if your dog is involved in an accident. Don't forget that you are responsible for his actions, even if you're not there.

So, to sum up, do not allow your dog out unless you are in attendance and in full control. You can never be sure what might happen if you are not there. Your dog may be taught how to behave whilst you are there, but his reactions may change dramatically if you're not there to guide him.

Rolling in Muck —

Rolling in muck is a most common and natural behaviour to dogs. Dogs who roll in muck do so most commonly in an attempt to mask their own smell by rolling in a stronger one, and thus disguising their whereabouts. In the wild, this type of camouflage is of great benefit to hunting, as smell is many animals' first line of warning about predators.

Owners who wish to prevent this smelly habit need to be very vigilant when out walking with their dog, as dogs who are prone to this behaviour seem to dive in suddenly without any warning. It is easier to prevent the behaviour before it happens than to catch it in the act (and prevention is more likely to have good effect). As with other problems that occur whilst you are out and about, if the pleasure of being with you outweighs all other pleasures, then you are 90% on the way to eliminating problems (see Reward Training).

Second Home

There is much pleasure and satisfaction to be derived from adopting a second-hand or rescue dog. I have had several second-hand dogs, and all have had problems to sort out. They came from varying backgrounds—some were mistreated physically, and some were mistreated through simple neglect; others were spoilt by misguided kindness, and one was simply thrown out to fend for himself on the streets.

Oscar was simply not the right dog for the owners who chose him. He is lively, bubbly, excitable, and fun-loving—all qualities that can be difficult to handle if you're not quite ready for them. His first adventure in my garden on his own for just ten minutes resulted in muddy holes all over, my washing literally torn from the line, and Oscar covered in mud. His long, silky coat was a disaster area. Many people would have gone berserk and sent him back to where he came from—

the rescue centre! But Oscar was lucky this time because all we saw was a wagging tail that said 'what's next on the agenda of fun!' So we cleaned him up, rescued the washing, and accepted that Oscar had a lot to learn about what was acceptable in our home. I must impress upon you that we did not go out yelling and cursing, telling Oscar off. What we did do on the next day was go into the garden with Oscar and show him what fun could be had chasing a ball and having a game with an old rag that we gave him to play with.

The moment I caught his eye gleaming towards the washing on the line, I squealed with delight to attract his attention to me and waved his toy about. He came bouncing over, the washing forgotten, and played with me and his toys. For several weeks I did not allow Oscar to play unattended in the garden. I went with him and showed him the correct way to behave. If for a second he showed interest in the washing or the flower beds, I acted like a football fan going wild with excitement over the ball or a toy. So Oscar learnt that it was much more fun to play with the things that I wanted him to play with, and that the other things were dull and boring in comparison (see Distraction Training).

I still occasionally catch that gleam in his eye as the washing dances temptingly in the breeze, and all I do is have another little session of excited play with his toys. The qualities that you must possess if you want to own a dog, and more particularly a rescued or second-hand dog, are kindness, commonsense, and most of all patience.

Some dogs are not sufficiently socialised and come to you frightened of their own shadow. They often shrink away from anything that they do not understand, or bark and show aggression. These dogs need the patience and kindness of a saint. It takes time and very careful planning to help these poor animals. Each new situation that you introduce to them must be pleasant, and be very gradually introduced. If, for instance, your dog is not used to traffic, start way back from the busy roads, and just sit with your dog far enough away for him to show no fear. Tomorrow you can go a couple of yards closer, and so on, building up day by day until the dog learns from your confident manner and gentle praise that there is nothing to worry about. If taken very, very gradually, most fears can be overcome. Never tell your dog off, as this will only prove to him that there must be something to worry about— otherwise why would you be upset? This will put you back to square one.

With a dog who is very fearful, I would not commence training when I first get him but would wait a few weeks until he has learnt to trust me in the safety of my own home and garden. I would use the first few weeks to teach him to play with me.

If he doesn't automatically play, I close my mind to the fact that he is an adult and pretend that he is a six-week-old puppy. I get down on the floor with him and teach him how to play. I commonly use a soft knotted rag or a ball, playing with it myself and inviting him to join me. I choose times to play when the dog is at his most lively, perhaps first thing in the morning or when meal time is approaching. If he does not want to play, I put away the toys and try again later or the next day. The toys are not left out in case he wants to play, for they are mine and he can only play if we play together. Sometimes it takes a chew bone or a sock full of dried liver to tempt a dog to play, but eventually every dog comes around, and even the most sober of characters can squeeze out a little enthusiasm when he's hungry. Once the dog will play, you can use it to distract him from a situation that might cause fear. Approach a situation from a good distance away and produce your toy, encouraging the dog to play. It takes away the intensity of the situation and helps the dog to deal with his fear (see also Play Training). For all specific problems with your dog, turn to the relevant sections, but always remember that the most important thing with a second-hand dog is developing a relationship with him before you start adapting his behaviour to fit your lifestyle.

One way to acclimate a new dog to his second home is with a nice grooming session. Photo by R. Pearcy.

Shaping

The term 'shaping' is a term which is much more widely used in the world of general animal trainers as opposed to dog trainers. People who teach dolphins use shaping methods all the time. Have you ever thought how to get a dolphin to jump through a hoop? You can't pick the dolphin up and throw it through the hoop and say, 'There, that's what I want you to do.' Dolphin trainers use a training programme that brings the animal nearer and nearer to the required task. Using rewards (fish in the case of dolphins), they gradually condition the animal's behaviour. For instance, each time the dolphins swim from left to right, the trainer blows a whistle and gives them a fish. The reward and whistle are given for that action only, and soon the dolphins learn what action is needed to gain a fish. This conditioning, or shaping, is taken further to get the dolphin to break the surface of the water and gradually go higher and higher to gain the reward.

Dogs also can be trained in this manner of gradually getting nearer and nearer to the goal by encouragement and reward. This type of training often gets better results than physical and negative compulsion methods, and a combination of gentle physical guidance together with shaping and rewards—be they food, toys, or play—results in the most reliable and happiest of dogs, and thus the happiest of handlers and onlookers. Dog training should be enjoyable for all, including the dog.

You can't pick up a dolphin, throw him through a hoop, and say, 'There, that's what you do when I say jump!' Dolphins are taught by shaping, and dogs can be taught in the same way.

Agility is a fun sport that can be enjoyed by all fit dogs and handlers, whether they be large, like this German Shepherd Dog, or . . .

Showing

Showing is the common term for the sport of exhibiting or demonstrating dogs in the competition ring, be it for their good looks or their ability to work.

AGILITY

Agility is a most exciting sport which can be great fun. A specialist club is your best bet for getting started, as you will need to teach your dog to master many jumps. Don't forget that control is one of the all-important factors in Agility. Dogs must be both fast and accurate, so teach basic obedience as well.

. . . small, like this Papillon.

CONFORMATION SHOWING

This is when dogs are taken into a ring and their various attributes are pitched against others, usually of the same breed. A judge is appointed to make his opinion as to which one is the nearest to the standards set down by the breed council. The classes are normally divided into various sections to deal with dogs of various ages from six-month-old puppies to veterans. If you are interested in showing your

Flyball can be great fun for both dog and handler, either for competition or just for pleasure and exercise.

dog in this way, it's best to join a ring-craft or breed club. They will show you how to stack your particular breed and

This fine Pekingese owned by I. G. Hankins demonstrates the sport of conformation.

advise you on how to enter shows. The national kennel clubs have a list of these clubs and should be able to give you the names of those clubs in your area.

FLYBALL

In Flyball competition, the dog is required to jump over hurdles, hit a lever that releases a ball, catch the ball, and race back to the handler. It is a most exciting team event, and again you need to join a club to become a member of a team.

FRISBEE®

Frisbee® is not quite so common in England as in America, where championships are held. The AKC can tell you how to contact clubs that specialise in this event.

OBEDIENCE COMPETITIONS

This is where dogs of all types compete against each other through various set exercises to determine which one is most obedient and can carry out the exercise in a precise fashion. Again, classes start with a beginner's standard, and you can work through to a very high level if

Top and Bottom: Teaching scent discrimination is fun and can develop the dog's natural ability to use his nose. This exercise is involved in British obedience from the third level onwards.

you have the time to train your dog to the high degree required. Clubs are a good idea to get your dog accustomed to working with other dogs around, but try to find one that specialises in competition work. If you are really keen, then you should get off on the right footing. Competitive obedience is great fun, and you will make many friends in the quest for the perfectly behaved dog. Remember that it is a sport, and the dog did not have the option to join—so keep it happy. We all, of course, like to win, and the competitive spirit will live on, but please remember that you are dealing with an animal, and we are very fortunate to be allowed such a wonderful relationship.

If your dog goes wrong in the ring, examine yourself and your training methods. Do not take out your frustrations on the dog. (If you are particularly interested in obedience

Obedience tests take various forms and are popular in many different areas of the world. Here a sit-stay is performed at novice level in Britain.

Sheepdog trials test a dog's instincts. Here a Border Collie expertly moves sheep at a herding trial.

competitions, please read my book *Happy Dogs—Happy Winners*).

WORKING TRIALS

Another competitive sport with some of the same exercises as obedience, working trials also incorporate jumps, tracking, and searching. It is usually a more relaxed sport in which qualification as opposed to winning is more the order of the day. Trials do tend to be worked over a few days, so you will need plenty of free time for this one.

Sit

Show the dog what you require from the sit command. Do not expect him to know automatically. Repetition and praise will result in a dog who is keen to obey every time—not just sometimes.

Just because he is a dog doesn't mean he comes ready and able to understand simple doggy commands like 'sit' and 'down'. It's amazing how many people say, 'He's a dog, so why doesn't he sit when I tell him?' But, I'm sure that you are not one of those people, otherwise you would not be reading this book! Timing is most important when teaching any task, and I strongly recommend that you read the section on timing first.

The sit position obviously is quite a natural position for the dog; and, with an incentive like his dinner, he can learn to respond to the command quite readily. But, by far the best method of teaching the dog to sit on command is by gently, physically showing him what you mean. With your dog under full control (i.e., on a lead), gently guide him to your left side, holding the lead in your right hand, close to the collar for the best control. Place your left hand flat on the dog's rump

If you are patient and train with kindness, your dog will be happy to sit in the position until you tell him to do something else.

and simultaneously raise your right hand up with the lead; push your left hand down and say the dog's name and the command 'sit.' Do not babble to him about the weather or the price of beef. Just give plain, simple, calm commands, followed immediately by gentle praise, so he knows you're happy, and then relax the lead, as the dog must not feel a tight lead when he is in the correct position. So it's right hand up with the lead, left hand down on his rump, 'Oscar sit; good boy; super dog!' Simple isn't it?

The secret is to make sure

that Oscar sits until you say he can move! Otherwise he is not obeying the command at all. So keep him in the sit for a few seconds only to start with, and then say, 'Good boy, that'll do,' and make him break the position. Thus, you told him to sit, and he sat; you told him to move, and he moved. He is now learning to obey commands when they are given and not to make his own decisions as to when that command ends.

Remember to be fair with your dog. If he looks tired or fidgety, break the exercise; but, you do the breaking so that he learns that commands must be obeyed but are fun to obey. Not only does this make him a well-behaved pet to be proud of, but some day that instant reaction could save his life.

The length of time the dog is required to stay in the sit position can be lengthened as he gains more confidence. Eventually you will be able to leave him and go into another room, and return to him still patiently sitting. But this takes time and patience on your part. You must be sure that he is absolutely certain that your command means what we know

it to mean. If you move away from him too soon, he will feel uncomfortable and will not understand that sit means 'stay there even if I am not there,' because his natural reaction of fear to the unknown and his desire to be with his family take over. Some dogs will bark or whine, but most will simply walk away from the uncomfortable feeling. So, take it step by step, slowly but surely, and give the dog no cause for concern.

If you do go too fast, too soon, you may in effect be teaching your dog to do the opposite of what you are trying to achieve, because, as I explained in the introduction, he reacts only to circumstances and triggers that he can understand or has been systematically taught to respond to. For a positive response, you must give every help to the dog so that he can understand (see also Timing, Training, Triggers).

Facing page: *Even a naturally dominant breed like the Bouvier des Flandres can be made to assume the sit position with proper training.*

Socialisation

A well-socialised dog can be left in any situation and will behave impeccably.

Socialisation is one of the most important factors in the upbringing of your dog.

Your dog needs to socialise with other dogs, people, and animals, and part of his socialisation programme should include going out into the town or city to learn how to deal with the noise and hustle of day-to-day life outside the safety of your home. A well-socialised dog is a happy dog.

I start as soon as possible to introduce my dogs to as many things and situations as I can. With a puppy, as soon as he is through his inoculations, I start gradually to introduce him to the big wide world. Even before that I will take him out in the car on short journeys, or to friend's houses, where I know there is no chance of infection. I cannot underline enough the importance of socialisation. Each time your dog encounters a new situation and learns to cope with it in a pleasurable controlled environment, he catalogues that situation and reaction in his brain for future reference. The more situations he learns to cope with, the easier it becomes for him to deal with new ones. Eventually your dog will be able to cope with almost anything that he is confronted with, and react favourably.

On the other hand, if you do not take the time or make the effort to socialise your dog, you are likely to have either a nervous, aggressive, or unpredictable dog. If you acquire your dog as an adult, it is not too late to start the socialising, but you may well have to take things at a slower pace, because he will have doubtlessly learned some less-than-desirable responses to situations, and those will be now catalogued in his brain. If

Training classes will help you to learn the art of control under a wide variety of circumstances.

There is perhaps no more perfect relationship than the one that can exist between child and dog, but both must first be properly socialised to each other.

this is the case, you need to take things slowly, introducing situations from a distance, and shaping your dog's reactions by reward and praise. The more traumatic your dog's experiences have been in the past, the slower you need to go. Be guided by his reactions, and help him every step of the way by being strong and positive and yet kind, gentle and understanding. Introduce one situation at a time and get good results before going on to another.

Dog clubs are great places for socialising your dog, but be careful not to sit next to an aggressive dog or handler, as dogs do learn from others. You don't want to give him bad experiences if you can help it, until he has learnt to cope a little more with life.

Speak on Command

You cannot show a dog how to bark in the same physical manner as you can teach him to sit. The way to teach speak on command is by shaping (see Shaping).

There are two things you can do, and I use both when teaching my dogs to speak. Each time the dog barks naturally I say, 'Good boy, speak,' instead of what most

Having your dog speak on command can be a good way to increase a dog's deterrent effect against intruders. Airedale Terrier photographed by S. A. Thompson.

say, which is 'Be quiet!'

I take my dog into situations which might entice him to bark. As soon as I hear a rumbling, I encourage him by saying, 'Good boy, speak!' I make sure that the situation will not cause distress to the dog or others, and I always make sure that I am in a position to give my dog confidence, i.e., by his side with my arm around his shoulders. As his rumblings or barks begin to subside, I say, 'Good boy, that'll do,' and turn him away from the situation and distract him. He learns that barking is allowed, but only under control, and when I say so. This exercise also helps to stop barking when you do not want it. Even with a trained dog, I never shout, 'Be quiet.' If a dog barks when I do not want him to, I say 'Good boy, that'll do,' which is my command for stop barking. When the dog is trained he will always stop barking quite happily on this command, content that he has made you aware of the situation to which he wanted to draw your attention, such as

someone at the door.

Another method of teaching the dog to speak, which I use alongside the former, is to tie the dog in a safe place and then talk and play in an excited manner just out of his reach. A dog who is always happy to be with you and enjoys a game will become excited and, almost always, will start to bark. At the slightest suggestion of a bark, you should start to encourage the dog by saying 'Good dog, speak,' whilst carrying on with the game. As soon as the dog starts to bark you can really go overboard with the command 'speak' and praise. At the slightest hint that the dog is going to stop barking, go up to him and say, 'Good boy, that'll do,' gently calming him with your hands.

Using the second method only tends to incite the dog into speaking for toys and attention, which in some cases can be a nuisance. Use the two methods together and the dog becomes accustomed to the command and its antidote.

—Submissiveness

Submissiveness is not normally a problem, except perhaps when the dog urinates when put into a situation that causes his submission.

Puppies are often submissive and show the classic submissive postures, including the crouching sideways approach, exposing the belly, and sometimes turning completely on their back. Puppies and young adults are most likely to show this behaviour when approaching other dogs or even humans.

If your pet is extremely submissive you can ease the situation by turning away so as not to give an eye-to-eye

It is most important that all dogs show submission to their owners. If they do not, the owner has little chance of being able to control his dog in a problem situation.

If the submissive dog goes wrong, do not confront him but guide him. Photo of Pharaoh Hound by V. Serbin.

confrontation, then giving the dog something positive to do that you know he can cope with. I had an experience with a young adult bitch who was extremely submissive and would urinate at the slightest thing. I took this little bitch into a hotel with me, and her immediate reaction was to jump excitedly on the beautiful white duvet cover on the bed. She would not normally have done this at home, but a different place and different situation can give you a different reaction (see Triggers). My immediate reaction, knowing that I had not taught her the 'off' command, was to reach out and pull her off. But as soon as my arm went out, I saw her go into the submissive posture. Any further confrontation with me would have resulted in a trickle of urine decorating the pristine duvet. So I turned away, hard as it was, and turned my back on the bitch. Then, in a light voice, I called the dog, and she trotted 'round to me. I praised her gently and calmly so as not to set off her submissive reaction again. The moral is not to confront submissive dogs but to guide them, giving them tasks to do that they are confident with. Keep your voice light and natural, and step by step your dog will learn to submit less and less.

A truly submissive dog rarely becomes aggressive or dominant, and he seldom becomes involved in fights with strange dogs. Even the most dominant dog recognises the complete submission of a submissive dog, and realises that the dog poses no threat to his position.

Submissive dogs can, however, develop certain reactions like barking at distant strangers or unusual objects, because of their fearfulness (see also Fearfulness).

Puppies learn submission at an early age from their parents. Submission is an important survival tool to wild canids. Photo courtesy of Barbara Lewis.

Supersense

Do dogs possess supersensitive powers? It is a subject of much discussion, and most doggy people have a tale to tell about it.

Dogs are far more sensitive to smell, sound, and fear than we are; so, in that respect, I think we can truly say that they do possess supersense.

But what about the more intriguing occurrences, like dogs who remain with their dead owners and dogs who travel miles to be reunited with their family? My story is a true one, and one that you may find a little spine-chilling.

When I was eighteen years old I had a little rescued mongrel called Guacha and together we set about house hunting because the flat that I then occupied left a little to be desired.

I had saved a deposit and had a secure job, so all that was left was to find a suitable home for myself, my dog, and two cats. Guacha and I looked at many houses, walking miles in our quest for our perfect home. We thoroughly enjoyed the task, and Guacha found great pleasure in running through the empty rooms and up and down the hollow stairs of these unoccupied houses. After a few weeks of searching, my excited estate agent told me he had found the very thing: a super little house with a walled-in yard, central heating, full modernisation—the works! I couldn't wait to dash over to see it. We collected the keys and took directions, and off we went with bated breath. As we approached I could see what the estate agent meant—it was a nice quiet area, and the house was in perfect repair.

I fumbled with the keys, convinced that I had found my dream home. I opened the door and stood back waiting for Guacha to rush in, but no. I glanced down by my side and there she stood, her hackles standing on end. A chill went

Dogs have amazing powers of perception. Siberian Husky surveying the landscape. Photo courtesy of owner S. Roselli.

down my spine. I tried to encourage her into the house but she dug her heels in and refused. I nervously entered the room alone. It was just as the agent had said, and I could see the perfect little yard out back through the window. Suddenly Guacha dashed in, still with hackles up and started tugging me back towards the open door. I went with her, half thankful, half annoyed. The house looked so perfect and yet had a strange eerie feeling. We left and returned the keys. I didn't explain what had happened to the estate agent, for I thought he would think I was nuts. But, Guacha obviously felt something that I was not sensitive enough to pick up. A spine-chilling experience indeed and one that I will never forget.

Another true story, also with a mind-bending feeling happened when I lived in my mother's house, just before I got married. I was alone in the house with my two dogs Guacha and Taffy, a crossbred Border Collie/German Shepherd Dog. Taffy was quite young but a real character. I had left the dogs in the lounge whilst I was upstairs making my bed. Suddenly I heard barking, at first I thought it was the two dogs playing, but then I realised that the bark was more of an alarm call. I went to the top of the stairs and saw Taffy standing barking to me. I then smelt a nasty acrid smell of burning. I rushed down to find that I had rather stupidly left a rack with drying clothes around the gas fire. The dogs in their game had knocked it onto the fire and it was smouldering. I rushed towards it and pulled it away from the fire, which of course allowed the oxygen in, and the flames roared up to the ceiling, and the room filled with smoke. I rushed next door and hammered on the door. My neighbour was a fireman, but it took an eternity for him to come. His small son who answered the door thought I was joking (I suppose it happens a lot when you're a fireman's son!) I finally assured him of the emergency, and his father jumped into action. I stood outside with Taffy while he went in. Suddenly Taffy dashed back into the house, ignoring my calls for him to come back. Seconds later he came out dragging the petrified Guacha by the scruff of the neck to safety. A few moments later my neighbour emerged. He was carrying the flaming clothes rack which he deposited in the garden. He went back in and dampened down the remaining flames. Thankfully not too much damage was done. He told me that Taffy had dashed through the smoke-filled room into another at the other side of the fire and dragged poor Guacha out. A truly heroic deed, and one I would not have thought possible had I not been there myself. Both of my stories are perfectly true, and whether they can be explained by natural or un-natural phenomena, they certainly show how wonderful and supersensitive the dog is.

Sighthounds, such as the Saluki, possess the keenest eyesight in the dog world. Photo by I. Francais of Saluki owned by Paula Clarke.

Tail Chasing ────

Tail chasing can result when a dog or puppy lacks sufficient environmental stimuli. Training is an excellent way to provide additional stimulation.

Tail chasing is a compulsive behaviour. It is often seen when a young pup is isolated from his litter mates. Normally it only progresses into adulthood when an active dog is deprived of sufficient stimulation, play, or diversity, and becomes bored. It is very commonly seen in zoo animals, together with pacing, biting of their own flesh, and other stereotypic behaviours.

So what starts off as an amusing antic can develop into an indication that not enough time is being attended to your dog's mental well-being.

It is, however, possible to teach a dog to chase his tail on command. Shape him by encouraging him each time he does it. Eventually he will learn to do it when told; and, as long as he has lots of other things to stimulate him and prevent him from getting bored, no harm will become of it.

Tail Wagging

Have you ever wondered why your dog wags his tail? I expect most people think that it's because he's happy, which is not quite correct. The dog wags his tail because he is in conflict with himself: he wants to go left, yet he wants to go right; he doesn't know what's going to happen next, and he is anxious

A dog wags his tail because he is anxious. This Bullmastiff wonders, 'What's next?' as owner E. Elitz approaches. Photo by I. Francais.

to make the right moves.

The faster his tail wags, the more anxious he is that things will go well, and he tries to anticipate what's next. Therefore, when we see a so-called happy wagging tail, which makes him look to us as if he's a happy dog, what he's really wanting is for the situation to level itself and to know what's next on the agenda! If you watch a submissive dog or a young pup, his tail might be wagging very fast, while at the same time he is urinating or squirming about on the floor. He's anxious and in conflict, wanting to know how to proceed, and is totally submissive. His anxiety is less easily concealed than in a more mature or dominant dog.

Very tiny puppies in the nest do not wag their tails. Tail wagging only starts when interaction between siblings and the bitch starts. The puppies, at about two weeks old, start to play and have mock fights for dominant positions in the nest. Then,

These Mastiff pups have reached the sibling interaction stage, and thus their tails will be wagging. Photo by R. Reagan of Mastiffs owned by Winterwood Kennels.

When a puppy is approached, he may be apprehensive, and his wagging tail will suggest his anxiety. Photo of American Cocker Spaniel pup by I. Francais.

when they go to the bitch to suckle, they have to lay very close to all those other pups with whom they have just been fighting. This proximity causes a little fear, and yet the desire to suckle is greater, so the pup becomes in conflict with himself and this is when the earliest tail wagging starts.

When we greet our dog after being parted, the dog approaches, tail wagging, looking upon us as top dog of the pack, the dominant party, and so he is in conflict—he wants to greet us and yet is slightly frightened or overawed by our superiority.

We do not like to think of our dogs as being frightened of us, but if we did not demand this respect then problems could arise, including aggression towards us.

Dogs also give off scents from their anal glands, and the tail wagging helps to spread the scent rapidly so that it can be picked up by other animals quickly, thus preventing unwarranted attacks, etc., as the scents are like odour messages to other animals.

Teaching Methods

There are many, many books written on dog training and they outline various methods of teaching set tasks such as walking to heel, sit, retrieve etc. Almost without exception, these methods will work. The first secret is understanding how the dog's mind works so that you can recognise when things are going right and, more importantly, when things are not going correctly. The second secret is timing, and knowing when the dog is becoming confused.

All dogs, just like us, are individuals. They learn at different rates and react in different ways. These differences are because of breeding and genetics, and upbringing (the way the dog has been moulded by his surroundings and the people and other animals he has been brought up with, the rules that have been set down to live by, and the dog's interpretation of those rules).

So most methods of teaching will work. My aim is to enjoy my dogs, and to teach others to enjoy theirs, too. I would never choose a teaching method that is harsh, cruel, or would cause physical pain or mental distress to my dog. I like my dogs to feel comfortable in my presence and able to relax, not to be tense and unsure.

I have had several dogs who came to me from previous homes, where they obviously had not the best of understanding. These dogs needed special care. I have written a separate section just for them (see Second Home).

But, all in all, most methods (many of which are explained in the various sections of this book) work for most dogs. The secrets are understanding and timing.

To learn more about these methods of training, you need to turn to the relevant sections in this book and possibly also read some other good books—

It is most desirable that owner and dog attend training class together.

and go along to a training class, as well. As with all other fields, there are good teachers, not so good, and downright terrible teachers of dog training. So ask around, as the best form of advertising is personal referral.

Thieving————————

Dogs are most resourceful, and they will soon learn ways to get what they want. In my early days, I lived in a ground-floor flat with my companions Guacha, a lively little bitch of undetermined heritage, and Taffy, a crossbred Border Collie–German Shepherd Dog. Both were delightful canines and full of character. My flat was rather small, and I shared a bathroom with other people in the house. The bathroom was upstairs, and the entrance leading to the stairs was in my lounge. The kitchen was at the opposite end of my flat, and the two dogs learnt that I was not always as vigilant at putting away food as I might have been. They also learnt that they would not be allowed to touch things that did not belong to them, such as food items and the contents of the kitchen bin, in my presence. But the trigger that said help yourselves was my hand on the door leading to the stairs. They became so conditioned to my hand on the

door meaning 'raid the kitchen' that I only had to reach towards it and they had gone. It took me some time in those early days to determine this behaviour pattern, as my steps coming back down the stairs were the trigger that told my friends to return to their previous positions, or to come and greet me (see also Triggers).

I didn't realise that my kitchen was being devastated, as I would return to my seat and only some time later would discover their misconduct. Sometimes I wouldn't notice it at all, if it was just a case of stealing a slice of bread or the cat's food. So quite unknowingly I conditioned my dogs to stealing—only in my absence.

How did I stop it? Well, it was quite simple. Once I had determined the behaviour pattern, I just closed the connecting door between my lounge and kitchen each time before I left the room. After some weeks, the dogs learnt that there was no point in dashing off as soon as my hand went to the door of the stairs, and I always gave them lots of praise and fuss when I came back in. They learnt that more reward was to be gained by waiting at the stairs door for my return. Some months later I experimented by leaving the kitchen door open again, but I made sure that there was no food around, just in case they clicked back into the previous behaviour. (I did it because I wasn't sure if it was my closing of the kitchen door that had become the trigger that made them wait for me at the stairs.) I waited at the other side of the door but heard no scuffles to the kitchen. My re-programming had worked. I had conditioned my dogs into receiving greater rewards for awaiting my return than for rushing to the kitchen.

So the way to stop thieving is first of all to prevent your dog from gaining access to the food, preferably by putting a barrier between the dog and the food, such as a door; or, if a barrier is not possible, removing the food, and, at the same time,

Dogs are naturally resourceful and will scavenge unless taught otherwise.

lavishly rewarding the desired behaviour.

The dog cannot be taught to refrain from thieving if he is continually given access to the things not allowed to him, as it in itself is rewarding the undesirable behaviour. He cannot understand if the chastisement comes afterwards, as it only serves to remind him of how strange we humans are—'they chastise for no apparent reason; maybe it makes them feel better.'

HOUSEHOLD ITEMS, CHILDREN'S TOYS, ETC.

This problem can be dealt with in much the same way as stealing food. A dog does not understand our concept of stealing as such, and, unless taught otherwise, any item left lying around is fair pickings. Children's toys seem to be the cause of most concern, as a dog's idea of playing with a toy is often to chew it up, and children somehow do not think that chewing is fair game.

Dogs should *never* be left unattended with children. For the safety of the child, more than for any other reason. In bringing up my son, I never left him unattended with any of my dogs. Even though they show great gentleness towards him, I have never considered it worth the risk—they are only animals after all, and we must never forget it, no matter what our emotions may tell us.

If you do not leave your dog with your child, then you are always in control. Your dog should be taught to leave on command, and then a careful eye kept on him at all times. Eventually he will learn it's not worth picking up the forbidden items, because he will always be told to leave them—the novelty soon wears off.

The same goes for any other household item. Use your commands. Either catch him before he gets to something that you don't want him to touch, or give the command 'come' and 'leave' if he has already got something. Don't lose your temper if he has picked up your best shoes, just call him to you, tell him to leave, and praise him for leaving. He will either drop the shoes and come or bring them with him. Either way you have the desired effect with a minimum of fuss. He will soon tire of picking up these items if it is not allowed to become a game. So be pleased with him, not angry. The first time you become angry over something like this, you are on the first step to his not wanting to come to you. He will probably try to get away and take whatever he's got in his mouth with him. So keep calm, use your basic training commands, stay in control, and don't forget that if something is so precious, you don't risk it, put it well out of his reach.

Teach your dog the household rules—but remember that if he has ever been allowed to thieve in your absence you may as well have given him a reward yourself.

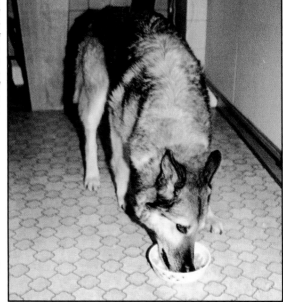

THIEVING IN YOUR ABSENCE

As I explained in the section on thieving food, the very fact of being able to thieve in your absence is a reward that says it's OK to do it. Nothing untoward happens. In fact, great pleasure can be derived from it. So sensible dog owners will learn to leave their dogs in a safe area when they are absent, to remove all items which might be of interest, and leave behind only items that they are happy for the dog to touch. Situations can be set up to frighten a dog into not going towards forbidden items—such as creating a loud bang as he touches it. But in my view these drastic steps should be taken only under strict supervision of an experienced dog trainer, as the timing has to be absolutely perfect so as not to distress the dog.

All in all, the best solution is prevention rather than cure, as in all other facets of dog training. So put away your valuables before you leave an animal in charge of your house.

Timing————————

Timing is the all-important element of dog training. Incorrect timing will invariably result in the dog's doing something completely different to what you were trying to achieve.

The dog cannot think as we do. He can only think of whatever is happening now. So, for instance, if you are to teach the dog to hold something in his mouth, first of all have a little game so the dog is happy, lively, and keen to participate in anything that might happen. Choose an article that is easy for the dog to hold, and one that is not injurious to him. Then open his mouth and gently place the article between his teeth, just behind his front canines, and say, 'Hold, good boy.' Take the article from his mouth and now the most important part, shut up! That is you, not the dog! If you take the article and then praise the dog, what is he to think? I will tell you: he thinks that, as soon

as the article is out of his mouth, you are happy! So 'hold' means 'spit it out,' which is exactly the opposite of what you were trying to achieve. Because of incorrect timing by means of praise after the event, the dog is totally wrong in our eyes, but totally correct in his own.

Correct timing applies to everything you wish to teach your dog. Commands and praise must be simultaneous with the act, never before or after. When people are training they sometimes get this first stage correct, more often by good fortune than anything else. Their problem comes when the dog starts to get the idea. Going back, as an example, to teaching the dog to hold, when the dog starts to get the idea and to venture towards the article on his own, then takes it in his mouth for a few seconds, the handler is so elated with the success that he overdoes the praise after the dog has delivered the article to him. It only takes one or two times for the dog to learn that the more abundant praise and fun comes when the article is not in his mouth. So next time he may well take the article but immediately spit it out and stand waiting for his praise, or he may not want to take the article at all, again expecting praise for his actions. The handler becomes puzzled, annoyed, and frustrated, and the dog is totally confused. If he could think like us, two or three escapades like this and he would be looking for another home! Thank goodness he cannot. What usually happens is the dog withdraws, and the handler becomes disheartened.

When praise and guidance coincide, they help to give the dog a clear picture of what is required from a given command.

Owners who find themselves in this situation find it virtually impossible to teach anything else because the timing is never correct, thus confusing the dog. In the end they give up and tell everyone that the dog is stupid. That same dog in the hands of a person who understands the concept of correct timing can in a few moments start to revert from the negative attitude (so long as the previous handler did not push his point too long and too hard), regain his confidence and start to 'switch back on.'

To sum up timing, if you are teaching your dog to carry out a task and he is not getting the basic idea within a few minutes, then look very carefully at the method that you are using to teach your dog, and most of all examine your timing. Are you actually teaching the dog what you think you are teaching him, or are you rewarding his actions at the wrong time?

Toys

Every owner should have some toys. No, this is not a printing error. I do mean every *owner*, and not dog. You must always make sure that the toys you have for your dog are yours and that he is invited to play with them when you say. This way he doesn't get ideas beyond his station and start to think that possession is nine-tenths of the law.

Let me explain. Dogs are pack animals and as such are constantly reaching for the top-dog position. This behaviour is most noticeable in the more dominant types but it is there lurking beneath the surface in all dogs, just waiting for an occasion to be released. By giving the dog his own toys and letting him demand where they are kept and when play should commence, he starts to be conditioned, by you, into thinking that he is the top dog and can control situations. I'm sure that I don't have to continue for you to understand

how this could, and in many cases does, get out of hand and lead to dominance in all aspects of day-to-day life. So you keep in charge of the toys and enjoy letting him share in the game.

There are many toys on the market, but be sure that the ones you buy are suitable for the size and temperament of your dog. Small pieces of rubber or plastic eaten by the dog, even if marked non-toxic, can lead to problems. Balls that are too small can get lodged in the throat and are virtually impossible to retrieve. Sticks are definitely a bad idea. Thousands, if not millions, of people go to the park and throw sticks for their dogs, but, if you had the misfortune to witness what I have seen, you would never throw a stick again.

I saw a young lady playing with a stick, throwing it for her German Shepherd Dog. They had been enjoying their game for some time. Suddenly, she

Make sure that your toys are safe for your dog, and remain in charge of them so as not to allow your dog to be in charge of you.

threw the stick, and it landed with its end in the ground. The powerful Shepherd was there almost immediately upon its landing. He came down on the stick, and the end went right through the roof of his mouth! We took him, with the stick still lodged in his upper palate, to the vet, and it took a major operation and weeks and weeks of pain and suffering before the poor dog recovered. A lesson was learnt by all. I NEVER throw sticks for my dogs. Use only the safest toys to play with your dog, and then put them away for your own safety and the health of the dog.

Toys can also be used as rewards in training exercises and in distraction training. I like to have what I call my recall toy, a special toy which can be produced from my pocket if the situation looks like it might become difficult. This toy means fun, excitement, play and love to my dogs, and I always leave them wanting more. My favourite article for my dogs is called Nylafloss®. It

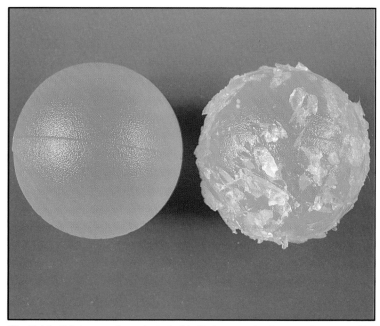

The Nylaball® is among the safest of all balls for your dog because he cannot bite off chunks of it. They are long lasting, and when your dog has worked one over well, simply replace it.

is a simple piece of thick rope, knotted at both ends, with tassels. Dogs love them. They are safe, and they can be washed in the washing machine. And whilst not a toy to be left with the dog, they make a great incentive/ motivation aid, as they fit into your pocket easily and can be produced for the dog at the most beneficial moment as a distraction from less-desirable actions. They have the added benefit of being good for the dog's teeth and gums, acting like dental floss. Any safe article which your dog enjoys can be used in this manner under your control.

Training

When embarking on training your dog, it is of upmost importance that you understand how your dog's brain operates. He cannot think like you and me; he can only respond to circumstances or instinct. It is far better to train a dog for reward, be that a treat or toy, or simply praise from you, than to continually give negative commands and hope or expect the dog to work out which part of what he is doing is correct or incorrect, particularly as we are so unreliable in our concept of what is right and wrong.

Here is how Oscar responded to the command 'down' when he jumped onto our seat with his muddy paws—because down *is what he understood by that command!*

Children can be quite good dog handlers, given that the animal has the correct temperament. But you should be very careful to not allow young children to be unsupervised with a dog.

For instance, if you are relaxing at the end of a tiring day with your dog curled up besides you on the bed, how is your dog to know it's wrong after a walk in the muddy woods to come in, just as tired, and try to curl up beside you again, covering your bed in mud. It may be very wrong in our eyes, but the dog cannot understand your anger, your outburst of 'Get off from here you filthy animal, you're covered in mud!' It only serves to remind the dog of what an unpredictable, unreliable, mind-changing animal humans are—you just cannot trust them. What about the family that takes their pet along to training classes, and teaches the dog to go down on command. Back at home the canine jumps onto a seat. 'Get DOWN!' says the owner, and our poor pooch lies down as good as gold, only to be grabbed by the scruff of the neck and plunged to the hard floor. What is our doggy friend to think? You say, 'Down.' He goes down. Oh, but today 'down' means 'get off.' So confusing! Dogs can learn that in certain situations a word can mean different things. But, it does not build up a good relationship of trust and understanding if we as intelligent humans cannot be as consistent as our canine friends.

The moral is be clear, be precise, show the dog calmly and patiently what is required from a word, and then stick to it, remembering to praise as soon as the dog shows the slightest understanding, and to be encouraging all along the way.

Dogs do not understand our language and have no capacity for lateral thinking. They can only learn an action in connection with a certain sound (word). The only meaning that the word or sound has to the dog is the one that he interprets from our corresponding actions. So, if our timing is slightly off, the word/sound that we are trying to get him to connect with an action can be interpreted by the dog as something completely different.

It is most beneficial,

and of paramount importance, that you establish a daily routine of training and stick to it as closely as possible. Obviously, things crop up in a household that have to take priority over dog training, but, if you can spare a little time each day to spend alone with your dog, to play, and to take him calmly through each exercise which you are teaching and also those which he already knows, your dog will very soon become very amiable and eager to learn. This constant reminding and

There are many devices to assist you in all aspects of dog training. This German Wirehaired Pointer holds his retriever-training buoy. Photo by I. Francais of Wirehair owned by J. E. Ford.

Top and facing page: *Big, strong breeds like the Rottweiler can pose certain demands, but correct technique can train even the most powerful of dogs.*

of intense work. Rather it should be fitted to what suits you. My daily routine incorporates lots of character building and some training, such as recall, drop on command, heelwork, and retrieve, whilst out on my daily walk.

At other times during the day—maybe whilst I am in the kitchen doing household chores—I may put my dog through sit–stays, down–stays, leave on command, or a little bit of precision work that I might need for the competition ring, all of which is accomplished in the small space of my kitchen. Do not get side-tracked if you are training in the house. For example, if the phone rings or someone comes to the door, always tell the dog that the exercise is over before attending to other matters. It only takes seconds to tell him that you have finished and to let him relax. But, if he's left in a sit, for instance, and you are no longer there to give him confidence, who can blame him for getting bored and moving off in the earlier stages of his training? And then you have given

relationship-building will develop to give you a dog on which you can rely. Without this frequent repetition and routine, the dog slips into other ways which come more naturally to him!

Training need *not* be an hour

yourself a problem. He now has gained relief (which is as good as praise or reward to a dog) for disobeying a command. He doesn't understand that we see him as disobedient, and will be extremely confused if we are angry with him. He won't have a clue as to why. If this unfortunate situation does happen, just go back to square one and re-train the whole thing, giving plenty of encouragement as you go. It seems a bit drastic with a dog who might have been already quite well trained, but it will save lots of frustration and confusion for both you and your dog (see also Intelligence).

TRIED IT ALREADY

This section is aimed at helping you to understand why certain training methods do not work for you. It is a reply to one of the most common comments in dog training classes, 'I have already tried that and it does not work.'

Most stable, sensibly bred dogs will start to show an understanding of an exercise that is being taught in the correct manner within a couple of minutes. It may not be

perfect, but you should be able to see some light at the end of the tunnel!

If the dog is totally confused after a couple of minutes of training, stop, and think carefully about what you are actually doing. The most common factor for a method of teaching an exercise not to work is timing. Timing is so critical. The dog, we must remember, cannot think

backwards or forward. He is reacting to what is happening now. So, for example, if you are teaching your dog to heel, and you check him into the heel position and shout, 'Heel,' in an aggressive manner, when he arrives in the correct position he will think that you are displeased with his being on a loose lead by your side. He cannot understand that you are cross with the action that occurred a fraction of a second before. So he becomes very confused and is progressively taught by bad timing that he may as well ignore the check on the collar because the handler is not pleased with whatever he does. Similarly, if the dog is being taught to hold something, many handlers fall into the trap of thinking that lots of praise for the dog after he has held and then given back the article will result in a good retrieve; but, remember, it's the thing which he is doing now that he relates with praise. So, in the dog's eyes, he gets praise for spitting out the article! Timing and thought are so important to good dog training.

Always look around when training the dog and consider what external factors may influence his reactions. If, for example, you always teach the sit in the kitchen, your dog may be relating that exercise to some feature in the kitchen and have difficulty understanding that the command means the same thing outside of that environment. Thus you must show him calmly and with care exactly what you mean, in differing surroundings. Dog owners who are struggling to train their pets often will say at the dog club, 'He does it at home,' or, 'He comes back when loose in the garden, but not when loose outside in the fields.' Your dog is not being naughty when he reacts in this way. He is just confused or blasé about your wishes. He understands the command under a certain set of circumstances only. So, to be sure of positive reactions to your commands, you should train each exercise under many different circumstances, and I mean train from scratch. Do not try to practice the finished exercise. Instead show the dog exactly what is wanted as if he had never done it before.

Once the dog is trained in

one situation, it becomes quicker and easier to teach him the exercise elsewhere. But, until you have done it, you can never be absolutely sure that the dog understands your commands fully.

Handlers who do competition work can come across the problem of the dog's performing flawlessly at home but in the show ring acting as though he never heard of the exercise. It is essential in these cases to set up a show situation and atmosphere very carefully and then to train the dog from scratch. Often shows supply a practice ring, which is an ideal ground for sympathetic training—do not forget to ask a friend or two to come and stand around to act as mock judge and steward, giving the finishing touches to the atmosphere. For the end result to be good, remember to *train*, not practice.

So if you have 'tried it already,' do not automatically blame the dog or the training method. Look long and hard at the way you are putting it over to the dog. Are you actually telling him what you think you are telling him in a way that he can comprehend? (see also Motivation, Teaching Methods, Timing, Triggers).

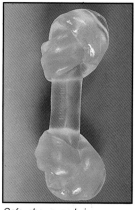

Safe chews and rings serve well as training rewards.

Travelling

Many dogs, unused to travelling, suffer from motion sickness—some because they are nervous about the experience, and others because there is too much excitement. It is quite rare for dogs not to overcome this problem if a regular training programme is followed.

If your dog is very ill, it is advisable to try some travel sickness pills along with the training. There are some very good herbal types on the market, available from good pet stores, or your vet may prescribe something for you. If you go to the vet, ask for the tablets that do not make your dog sleepy in order for your training programme to be more effective.

Introduce your dog gradually to the car by first of all taking him to sit in it with you, without the engine running. Once he is happy and confident, start the engine (not in a closed area of course!) and just sit with him and reassure him that everything is OK. Once this stage is confidently achieved, you can try a short journey. If possible, ask a friend to drive so that you can concentrate on ensuring your dog's peace of mind. Gradually you can increase the length of journey. With excitable dogs, try to avoid busy roads to start with as the motion of cars passing by tends to make them worse. Keep giving the tablets before each journey for a period of time, and then try a short journey without and see how you go. Do not forget to read the instructions on the pack to make sure that you give the tablets in plenty of time before the journey starts.

Some dogs do find it very difficult to adjust to the motion of a car, just as some people do. You may find that your dog reacts differently if heavy rain is lashing down or water is splashing up from the road. These are things that the dog

Teach your dog to enjoy the car, and always make sure that there is plenty of ventilation, even on a cool day.

finds difficult to comprehend, but, with gentle and gradual conditioning, most dogs accept our modern way of life quite well.

You may find it beneficial, particularly with excitable dogs, to teach them to lie down so that they cannot see the movement of other traffic, which can also be achieved by transporting them in a covered cage.

If your dog is an excitable traveller (some dogs dash around the car barking and jumping from seat to seat), it is best for the safety of those in the car that the dog be restrained in some way. A dog guard or cage is the best idea if your car is big enough. A cage can be covered with a sheet and, in most cases, this will calm the dog down tremendously. Many dogs become most excited when they reach the destination. They anticipate a good run or a game, which happens more particularly when the dog is taken in the car regularly to a place where he is let out. You can relieve this problem by reversing that situation, e.g., by taking him with you in the car frequently but not letting him out as soon as you stop.

If your dog has come to expect freedom each time the journey ends, it can take a lot of time and patience to inform him otherwise—but it's worth persevering. The more you go out in the car, the quicker he will learn that the end product is not necessarily entirely for his benefit. Teach him to be in the car whilst it is stationary and be happy to stay in it while you get out alone. It does take time.

If you do not have the problem, don't let it occur. Make sure that you take your dog out in the car as much as possible, thus making it a normal part of life and not an exciting merry-go-round to the park.

If you are travelling to somewhere where you will have to leave your dog in the car, think very carefully beforehand. Is he happy when left in the car or will you return to find the upholstery and seatbelts chewed? Will you be parked where other dogs might try to say hello to him and scratch your car with their claws? But, most importantly, will he be too hot if left in the sun in a parked car? Many dogs die needlessly every year because owners do not realise the tremendous heat generated in a stationary car, even in the weak winter sun. So please, please do not be like the owner of two Poodles I saw at a dog show. The police were informed by concerned bystanders, that although the owner had only been gone 30 minutes and the windows were open a little way, the dogs were in great distress from the heat. The police arrived in minutes, but those minutes were too long for the poor Poodles who were literally baked alive. The owners returned to find a smashed window, some very irate bystanders, a police charge, and, the most upsetting part, two dead Poodles. So please think very carefully before leaving your dog in the car, even for just a few minutes.

Crates help to make travelling safe, and dogs enjoy the security that they offer. Owner K. Baronowski leads her Italian Greyhound into the crate after the show. Photo by I. Francais.

Treats ——————

A balanced diet is of the upmost importance for dogs, just as it is for all animals. Treats can be given but should not be included in the daily balance and not given in excess of the manufacturer's recommendations. Treats can be used in training or just to make you feel better. Be very careful if you give treats that you don't end up giving this luxury each time your dog demands. Not only is it bad for his figure but also it is bad for his behaviour. A dog who gets food on demand may soon become a dominant or aggressive dog, so be on your guard. You decide when treats will be given and don't be swayed by

Your dog must be taught to understand that humans should be allowed to eat in peace—even when not at the table.

The endearing look of the puppy makes giving extra treats hard to resist.

those big brown eyes. I have a routine of giving bedtime biscuits. My dogs' other treats come in the form of play, training, or exercise throughout the day. Each night, before I turn in, I check that each dog is warm and dry and give them a hard biscuit—the type that they can crunch to help keep their teeth healthy and clean. This is my way of checking that all is well, and I feel better if I have not gone empty handed—well I am human as well you know!

Seriously, treats for dogs, like sweets for children, are not necessary, but we do derive pleasure from the giving. But give in moderation and keep to the healthiest type, OK? (see also Diet, Feeding, Reward Training).

Tricks

Teaching a dog tricks or party pieces involves the same process as teaching anything else. Timing, understanding, motivation, and a clear view of what you are trying to achieve are always the essential components.

You start off by showing the dog what you want from him and giving him a reward for doing it. Say you want him to shake hands (paws), having already taught him the basic exercise of sit, you sit him in front of you, show him a titbit

To play dead can be taught as an extension of the down, with caring, patient training.

Top and bottom: By gradual shaping and motivation, your dog can be guided into various manoeuvres which are fun and impressive to others.

a hoop, you don't start off with it two-meters high! Start on the ground, giving him a command, guidance, and reward, and then very gradually lift the hoop higher, centimetre by centimetre, always rewarding his actions.

All tricks that are within the dog's bodily and mental capabilities can be taught this way—with patient, motivated perseverance. Enjoy your dog, we might see you in the movies yet!

or toy, gently lift a paw from the ground giving a trigger command, such as 'paw' or 'shake hands,' and whilst his paw is in your hand give him his reward. Repeat often, and he will soon learn that to get the reward he must lift his paw.

Other tricks are taught more by shaping. If you want to teach your dog to jump through

Triggers

The dog's brain works like a catalogue or computer: you input the correct information, in a way that it can understand, and then, when you press those 'keys' or triggers at a later date, the correct response comes out—usually! I say 'usually' because a dog is, of course, an animal and sometimes needs motivation to respond to those triggers. But, more often than not, an incorrect response from the dog to the pressing of a trigger (or a command or signal) is caused by handler error or incompatible surroundings. When we teach a dog a command and its meaning, there are very many factors to consider, like the surroundings, the distractions, the passive distractions (distractions we don't realise are there), and the frame of mind of both handler and dog. Therefore, for a perfect response to your trigger (command), you need to teach the dog all exercises and

actions from scratch, and in many situations. This way you will ensure that, after a time, the dog will understand the command for the meaning that you have given it.

Many other less-obvious triggers happen in daily life, but an obvious one is the postman's van. A simple shutting of the door or even the approaching engine triggers the alarm bark response. We accept and understand this particular reaction, but others are much more subtle and more difficult to detect.

Triggers can be created quite unknowingly just by sheer coincidence. For instance, a dog may have been startled by a man in a yellow coat, and then each time he sees a yellow coat he is spooked. He can even go to the stage where he is spooked by anything large and yellow, yellow being the trigger that provokes a reaction.

You may have lost your temper with the dog on entering

a particular room, and there after your entry into that room sends him running, another involuntary setting off of a trigger. Trauma often provokes the most obvious and extreme responses that can last a lifetime.

Triggers can work in sequence, too. For instance, a dog can be taught by repetition, praise, and good timing to jump a series of hurdles in a set pattern. When sufficient training is provided, each jump sets off the trigger in the brain for the next.

You may notice when out walking that your dog will be inquisitive about the same places each day, not just because of the smells and odours he picks up—although they in themselves are a trigger—but it's the appearance and the position of that corner or alley, seen on a regular basis, that triggers the interest to explore.

And so, it is the correct application of trigger-provoking actions or commands that gives us a well-trained dog. We shape the dog first of all by showing him what we want and then slowly and gradually removing

The dog reacts to all sorts of outside stimuli, so it is important to train in many different situations to ensure that your dog understands your command at all times.

some of the aids, at the rate that the dog is learning, until the dog is able to associate a trigger (command or signal) with a certain action. To keep the dog in perfect 'trigger reaction', we need to remind him regularly by giving him all of the aids, i.e., showing him again and again, with gentle manipulation and guidance, what we want from a given command. He will enjoy doing it if given sufficient motivation. It is important to read the sections on timing and motivation to understand how to teach the dog to respond to the triggers or set commands.

Unpredictable Behaviour

Though a difficult subject by definition, most unpredictable behaviour patterns are fairly predictable to a trained observer. Some breeds are more difficult to read, as their facial expressions and body postures are less obvious. But normally a professional dog trainer worth his salt can detect the slight indications that are the tell-tale signals.

If you have a dog whose behaviour you find difficult to predict, you must make a study of his behaviour patterns, analysing what happens just before and just after he reacts. I was once called out to help a family who owned an English Bull Terrier. He was extremely unpredictable, and yet when we analysed his behaviour, he was most predictable. The problem was working out the very second that he was going to react, in his case, to attack. His owner, a lady, and her 13-year-old daughter lived in fear of his

every move, and he was in total control of the household. He was a very powerful dog who had manipulated the two women into bowing to his every whim—a very dangerous situation.

It started with his demanding play, food, and outings. Because he was a puppy, his ways were quite endearing and so were encouraged by the household. He was dominant as a puppy and would grumble if the ladies were not in their places when he wanted to play. Not seeing any danger and enjoying the character of the dog, the two women entered into whatever game he demanded, whenever he demanded it. Additionally, the young girl was out at school all day, and the woman was out at work. The dog spent many hours alone and developed many compulsive behaviour patterns—tail chasing, pacing, and throwing his toys to bang on a hollow wall. He was bored. He was dominant. And in both mind and body, he was in sole charge of the household.

Each evening when the family had eaten their meal (after feeding the dog first as he demanded), the dog would play with his toys, insisting that the family join him. Occasionally he would settle for a nap, and then suddenly jump up and stand over one of the poor ladies, growling with fangs displayed. If they attempted to move, he would bite them, sometimes drawing blood. At other times he would leap into the doorway, preventing the ladies from going through and leaving the room. The dog at this stage was far too strong and powerful

for these dainty ladies to do anything but obey him, a terrible situation to find yourself in.

Hopefully none of you who are reading this section have such a huge problem. If you do, I suggest that you get professional help straightaway, before someone gets injured.

The guideline to follow with dogs who show unpredictable behaviour is that there is one thing that *is* predictable—the chances are that they will do it again. So do be aware and always on your guard. Be ready for action should the need arise (see also Aggression, Distraction Training, Dominance).

Bull Terriers and other bull-and-terrier types are known for their proud ways and fearless attitudes. Owners must be sure to keep the upper hand on these dogs. Photo by I. Francais of Bull Terriers owned by Des Jardines.

Fun and exercise with your dog is a quality way to maintain his mental, as well as physical, well-being. Australian Shepherd enjoying a game of Frisbee*. Photo by I. Francais of Aussie owned by Solinsky.

Unusual Behaviour

Chasing shadows, following lights, pacing up and down, and all manner of strange behaviours can be exhibited by our dogs. Most of these behaviours are either taught without our realising (see Passive Training) or derive from compulsive behaviour caused by boredom, with pacing and tail chasing perhaps the most obvious of them (see also Compulsive Behaviour, Tail Chasing).

You may also classify the sexual mounting of people's legs, cushions, etc., as unusual, although to the dog it is quite normal. When a dog is growing up in the litter, there are a few weeks in his life that are critical to this type of behaviour. From around one to three months, the young pup is recognising his own species, and any other species which are around—be they human, feline or other—become part of the pack and, therefore, a possible sex partner. As dogs grow up, they regard humans

as part of the pack, but a member that is never sexually available, as we do not give the correct erotic aromas. As time goes by and the poor dog does not get a chance to do what comes naturally, he may be sent into a frenzy of sexual frustration that means he mounts the nearest thing that is part of the pack. The way to deal with this behaviour is to

Puppies in particular are prone to exhibit what we humans might label as unusual behaviour. Old English Sheepdog pup photographed by R. Pearcy.

remove him and show your disinterest. He doesn't deserve a good hiding or any other physical or verbal abuse—after all *you* dictated this life of celibacy for him. He will learn as he grows older that you are not a suitable sex partner, don't worry.

Chasing lights and shadows is usually a passive-training problem. All animals are naturally attracted to movement, light, sound, etc. What normally happens is that when a pup first shows a reaction quite by chance, everyone thinks it's funny, and our amusement is taken as praise. It doesn't take very long for the dog to be obsessed by this fun activity, and then it can become a problem to the household.

The habit can be broken by transferring his obsession to something more appropriate, such as a toy. Obviously every situation is different, and you need to adjust your reactions accordingly. The general idea behind it is that each time the series of events leads up to the dog's compulsion, you deny him the actual thing, say the light, and produce a toy instead. Make a big fuss of the toy and play with it yourself (see Play Training). Deny the dog the pleasure of the light and continue to play with the toy. Set this situation up many times, as compulsive training is obsessive and can take some getting through. Eventually, by being denied the obsession and a great fuss made over the substitute, headway can be made.

The factor which makes it difficult is that, each time the dog is allowed or achieves his obsession, the very act of doing so gives him pleasure, and so is reward enough for him to want to keep doing it, so denial and another object to re-focus his energies on is the most effective way to tackle the problem.

-Urinating Indoors

Most puppies do not gain full control of their bladders and bowels until at least three months of age. If you experience real difficulty housebreaking your adult dog, a trip to the vet is a good idea. Photo by R. Pearcy.

Once started, indoor urination is quite difficult to stop because the faintest odour can linger, sending a message that tells the dog to do it again. Most problems of this type are covered in my section on housetraining, but sometimes it is more of a sexual habit than a housetraining problem. On the whole, dogs who are well exercised and have been carefully trained will never develop this distasteful habit; but, occasionally dogs—males in particular—will take to marking their territory indoors.

Often, if caught in the act and immediately put outside, a dog can be broken of the habit before it gets a hold. More often than not, the dog understands that it is not acceptable in your presence, but nothing untoward ever happens when you are not there, and so, because the act brings relief from frustration, it is a reward in itself, and he will carry on marking in your absence.

If you can set up a situation where your dog thinks he is alone, but where you can see him, you can dash in and stop him in the act. This situation, set up enough times, will make him aware that you could be there anytime and so remove the pleasure from the act. This, however, is not always possible. Also, if trying it, your timing must be perfect. It is no use rushing in after he has finished, as he just won't understand your annoyance. There are various sprays available which can be used to deter your dog, or it may be

simpler to remove him from the situation in which he does his dastardly deed, thus eliminating the problem.

Sometimes very submissive or young dogs will have the reaction of urinating when submitting, and they are unable to help themselves. You can help to alleviate their anxieties and so reduce the problem that most will grow out of, given time (see Submissiveness).

Dogs who are approaching the end of their lives sometimes suffer from kidney problems. It requires a vet to diagnose if there is a medical problem. Likewise, if your dog should suddenly start to urinate in the house (more than just one accident), after being a clean dog, then check with your vet, as he may have a bladder or kidney infection that can be soon cleared up with the correct medication.

Visitors

If a young pup is introduced to visitors and strangers at an early age, there is rarely any problem of aggression or fear. The more common problem is, to put it bluntly, that the dog is just 'a pain in the neck.' He does not sit still, pesters the visitors, and all in all is a great distraction and nuisance. It is not the dog's fault, I might add, for he just wants to make friends.

The basic rule is to teach your dog all of the good control exercises, e.g., the sit, down, and bedtime. Once your dog understands these simple commands, you can use them whenever the need arises.

Make sure that your dog has been well exercised before the arrival of your visitors, so that a pain in his bladder is not the cause of his itchy feet. When you are in the process of training your dog, it will be necessary to keep him on a lead when visitors come, so that greater control can be

The dog should be introduced to visitors, young and old, early in his life. In this way, he will not come to see them as threats.

exercised. Keep calm and do not be embarrassed by the fact that you are training your dog. In a few months, your friends and acquaintances will be complimenting you on the behaviour of your dog, and you will be oh so proud.

It is worth having a little patience and determination. Allow your dog to greet the visitors but prevent him from jumping up. Keep him by your side and calmly and quietly insist that he behave, using the exercises that you have already taught him. Young dogs may find it difficult to sit still if they are not tired, so just do a little social training, and then let them out in the garden to relax and play whilst you chat. If your visitors stay long enough, bring the dog back in and once again control him by your side. Allow him to greet the people quietly, and then insist that he must sit or lay quietly by your side. It may take a little time for you to gain control. The secret is to win, but nicely. As the dog matures, he will learn to emulate this acceptable behaviour and will be a perfect host! Your friends will pretty soon forget all of your training, hard work and perseverance, and ask where they might purchase such a well-behaved pet.

——Walking to Heel

Walking to heel does not come naturally to a dog. If you watch a pack of dogs, they do not walk side by side. But, in our community and lifestyle, it is important that our pet can walk by our side so as not to cause problems to other people. Preferably he can do it without pulling our arms out of their sockets.

The typical sight in a dog club, once a new dog owner has learnt to use certain commands to get his dog to heel, is the following: the dog and handler walk around, and the dog begins to pull; after a little while, the handler realises and wrenches the dog back, yelling 'Heel,' irrespective of what the dog is doing. Whether the dog ends up in the correct place or not, the handler follows it up with 'Good boy,' as he was told by the instructor. If you recognise yourself and your dog at this point, I suggest you read the section on timing, before going any further.

An added incentive of a toy or treat will help you to keep control. Keep your dog happy and—who knows!—you could end up winning competitions.

There is only one good reason for a dog to want to walk by your side in the heel position, and that is because it is pleasant and comfortable for him to do so. If the dog experiences a harsh voice and unpleasant manner, coupled by a wrench 'round the neck and the handler gasps out that command 'Heel,' well, I would not want to stay by your side either! So how do we make it pleasant for the dog to want to be there?

The dog can learn nothing if the lead remains tight all of the time—except to pull against it! If you are starting off with a young pup, you can use your charisma to keep him where you want him! The earlier you start, the better; and, if you are in the fortunate position of reading this book with your newly acquired eight-week-old pup, you need never be pulled at all.

The first step is to get your young pup used to having a lead and collar on. This should not be a traumatic event, but done gradually with fun and love. I start by playing on the floor with the lead and collar before it ever gets attached to the dog. Gradually the dog starts to associate fun with the lead and collar, and I begin to mould his behaviour, still encouraging the pup to play on lead. I progress slowly, at the

pup's own pace, and eventually progress to the stage where a little pull on the collar indicates to the dog that he can come and play or have love. So a little check on the collar is always associated with pleasure!

Once the pup is happy and confident, you can start to shape your sessions into a teaching programme.

If you are starting with a very small pup, stay down at ground level, i.e., on your knees, as you manoeuvre him into the heel position, using the lead or a toy as a lure. You can progress to standing up when he is confident.

Using a toy or Nylafloss® hold the puppy on the lead and play with him and his toy or the lead. Gently manoeuvre him onto your left-hand side whilst still playing with him, and take a couple of paces with your dog (somewhere near to the position you will want him to be in when he is older). Couple this with a very happy light command of 'Heel.' After you have been doing this for a few days, you can use the toy as a tease and as motivation as you take one or two steps, giving that same happy command of 'heel.' Then throw the toy for the pup and have another game. The one or two steps can be extended to three or four the next day, and in no time at all your young pup will be walking to heel and enjoying it. Do not try to go too fast. Remember that there is plenty of time if you start when the pup is still young. Within a few weeks your pup will be happy to walk by your side as the command 'heel' triggers nothing but pleasure. This method of puppy training will also stand you in good stead should you want to go on at a later stage into training for competitions.

Top and bottom: There is nothing more pleasing than being able to have complete control of your dog in a public place.

Working Dogs

Over the years many of my clients have called for help because their dog was out of control. In most cases, the dog in question was a member of a working breed. These breeds have been bred over generation upon generation to work for the human race until told to stop. If they are thrust into the life of a lapdog, it is no wonder that they have difficulty adjusting to such a lifestyle. Border Collies are bred to run up and down hills all day, come rain, hail or snow. If they are asked to sit still all day, bound by four walls, waiting for the return of their master, I think that it is asking rather a lot. As a breeder of collies from working lines, I always ensure that my pups go to a home where the owner will at least do some formal training, competition work or agility, etc., so I know that each dog's very active brain will have something with which to occupy it.

Even if you do remember a working

A true working dog, the Rottweiler of the past was a cattle drover, while the Rottie of today is a premier guardian.

The Australian Kelpie is a tireless herding dog. Photo by I. Francais of Kelpie owned by R. Bauer.

dog who was the nice, quiet playmate of your childhood, it does not follow that he is whom you will get today. Just because Guide Dogs for the Blind Associations frequently use Labradors and other retrievers for their nice placid guide dogs, it does not follow that the one you will get will be quiet. Many retrievers are bred to work in

the field to the gun. In general, the G.D.F.T.B. breed their own particular lines to get the specific type of dog that they need—and even then, many of the progeny never make the grade. Those who do become guide dogs experience two full years of concentrated training, all day, every day—much more than your dog is likely to get in

Among his many other tasks, the German Shepherd Dog has served as a rescue dog as well. Photo by A. Wintzell.

a lifetime. So do not be fooled into thinking how nice and intelligent these dogs are, it takes a special sort of handler to work with a lively animal, and a lot of good handling and perseverance to achieve what you see in field trials or at Crufts.

Buy a working breed by all means, but be ready for some hard work. If you have already got one, then resign yourself to the fact that you have undertaken to have an intelligent dog who needs to have both brain and body exercised sufficiently.

Join a club and get involved with other working-dog people. You never know, we might see you winning red rosettes before long. It's great fun, if you do not weaken as they say.

Worms

With the guidance and supervision of a vet, all dogs should be regularly given a course of worming tablets or liquid to rid them of any parasitic worms. 'Regular' means about twice a year for a normal healthy adult, and every four to six weeks for a growing pup. The most common worms found in dogs are roundworms, although occasionally tapeworms are prevalent.

External warning signs often appear. In puppies, a pot-bellied look is usually a tell-tale sign; in adults, ravenous appetite with loss of weight and in extreme cases vomiting are cause for concern. Watch out for fleas too, as they are part of this vicious cycle which will prevent your dog from being in peak condition. Many brands of pills and potions are generally available in pet stores to rid our canine friends of these parasites; but, if in doubt, always consult your vet.

With the guidance and approval of your vet, all of your pets should be wormed when a new dog or cat is introduced to the family to ensure that the new arrival does not infect all the others.

Young Dogs

Young dogs bring their own special problems as they grow from puppyhood to adolescence, and on to adulthood. They are learning all the time and, as you might say, testing the water. Dogs, in particular male dogs, but often bitches too, are striving to be top dog. Some try harder than others. Some are naturally submissive, and others have a definite dominant character. Some are placid, but most are lively. Like young people, young dogs strive to succeed. They want to fit into society but have to be educated and shown the way. They learn rapidly, and the more we teach them, the more they seem capable of learning. They soon pick up bad habits if allowed to do so, but equally they can easily be taught the correct way to carry on, through calm and quiet training. Young dogs are fun to own, and, if you are patient, you can see them progressing and maturing into a

pleasurable animal to live with, provided that you give them the correct guidelines in a manner that they can understand (see also Training, Triggers, Timing, Shaping).

Sometimes older or busy people find it hard to cope with young exuberant dogs, and they might find their lifestyle more suited to owning an older pet—rescue centres can often help you find an older dog. For most people, a young dog is a pleasure, and man and dog can enjoy fitting into each other's lives. Remember always to stay in control, making the decisions and not allowing your dog to make demands. Whether he is a large or small breed, a dog who has been allowed to rule the roost can develop into a real problem as he matures. You must remain top dog.

Feed yourself and your family first, (top dogs always get the best pickings); choose where your dog will sleep and don't be afraid to move that

Active and inquisitive, young dogs can be very demanding but highly enjoyable.

place when you choose to. On a regular basis, clean out your dog's bed, move him from it, and sit in it yourself, if you want—all of these actions tell your dog that you are the top dog and he is being allowed in his bed by you. Don't allow him to have sleeping areas that you cannot get to, as only the top dog has exclusive bed areas. Play with your dog but do not allow him to hoard the toys.

The toys must belong to you and he can have the pleasure of playing if he's invited. You should regularly make sure that you can take away your pet's food while he is eating, and also bones or chews.

Following these basic rules will prevent the young dog's ever believing that he is in charge. There are other rules to follow, too. If you are aware that your dog is particularly dominant or of one of the more dominant breeds, read the section on dominance.

Grooming is also an important part of a dog's daily routine and as such should form part of yours, too. It's a good time to check him over and make sure he accepts your handling him (see Grooming).

There seems to be a great deal to remember, but it can soon fit into any daily routine. Dogs like routine and are happy and most reliable when they can become accustomed to your ways.

It is not advisable to take on a young dog or puppy if you are out at work all day or live a very hectic lifestyle which may exclude the dog. A bored dog is a problem dog.

Conclusion

Author Angela White with her dog Oscar.

Zesty, zealous, zany: three Z's by which many dogs can be addressed. If you have read all of the sections of this book which relate to understanding your dog, such as motivation, timing, playing, shaping, etc., you will now know how to have a dog that can be full of zest and joy of life, and yet still be controlled and an example to the dog-owning public of what can be achieved with a little patience and understanding. All dogs are trainable to varying degrees, depending on their breeding and background, and also depending on your

Through play and caring, shaping and training, your dog can be full of life, yet controlled and admired.

relationship with the dog and your ability to put things over to the dog in a way that he can understand. Your timing must be 'spot on,' and the more intelligent and quick the dog is, the better the trainer you must be to achieve your aims.

Having read this book, you may now be filled with enthusiasm to go on to bigger and better things. There are many fields which you can investigate. People who enjoy training their dogs often like to take the next step from pet training and go on to competitive obedience, and this would seem to be the natural progression. There are also many other avenues to explore such as search and rescue, trialing, cart or sled racing, agility, frisbee, showing, etc.

Most of all, it is important that you enjoy your dog. Read and re-read the sections in this book which are relevant to you, and you will also find benefit in reading some of the sections which you may feel are less appropriate, in so doing expanding your knowledge of your canine companion. Understanding is enjoying, and remember, if your dog goes wrong, think 'Why?' Not 'Wallop.'

INDEX

Adolescence, 15–16
Aggression, 17–22
Aggression, fear and, 18
Agility, 181
Appetite, 23
Appetite boosters, 23
Attack dogs, 103
Bark on command, 193–194
Barking, 24–28
Bedding, 82
Beds, 82
Bedtime, 29
Biting, 31–33
Biting the lead, 33
Biting, play, 18, 32
Blindness, 61
Boarding kennels, 123–126
Boredom, 54
Breeder responsibility, 36–37
Breeding, 34–37, 137
Bucket collar, 32
Cages, 38–39
Castration, 136
Chasing, 40–42, 238
Check chains, 83–84
Chewing, 43–47
Children and dogs, 48–49, 134
Classes, 50–52
Classes, training, 211
Clubs, 50–52
Collars, 82–83
Come command, 160
Compulsive behaviour, 53, 202, 234
Conditioning, 178
Conformation showing, 181–182
Coprophagy, 54
Correction, delayed, 13, 171
Corrective training, 11, 14
Crates, 38–39
Crossing roads, 55–56

Deafness, 61
Destructiveness, 38
Diet, 57–58, 110, 228
Diet, coprophagy and, 54
Digging, 59–60
Disabilities, 61–63
Disabled owners, 62–63
Distraction training, 64–67
Dominance, 68–70, 71, 229, 234-235
Down command, 71–75
Down, instant, 160–162
Eating grass, 76
Elderly dogs, 140–141
Elizabethan collar, 32
Emotions, 12, 45, 115, 118
Energy, 77–81
Enthusiasm, 151
Equipment, 82–86
Euthanasia, 141
Excitement, 87–88
Exercise, 28, 89–91
Fear, 176–177
Fear biting, 18
Fear of traffic, 56
Fearfulness, 92–94
Feeding, 95–96
Feeding schedule, 57
Fight-or-flight impulse, 13, 94
Fighting, 97–99
Fleas, 249
Flyball, 181
Frisbee®, 182
Grass eating, 76
Grooming, 86, 100–102
Guarding, 103
Guide Dogs For The Blind Association, 90
Habits, bad, 64
Halter-style collars, 85
Head collars, 85

Heel, 154
Heel command, 243–245
Housetraining, 104–107
Howling, 108
Hyperactivity, 57, 78, 109-111
Inoculation, 112
Instant down, 160–162
Intelligence, 113–117
Jealousy, 118
Jumping up, 119–121
Kennels, 122–126
Lead training, 244
Leads, 82–83
Learning, 12
Leave on command, 127–128
Licking faces, 129–130
Misbehaviour, 13
Motion sickness 224
Motivation, 81, 131-133, 151
Mounting, sexual, 237
Mouthing, 134–135
Neutering, 136–37
Newbould, Tom, 7
Nylafloss*, 159, 215, 244
Obedience competition, 182–185
Obesity, 138–139
Old age, 140–141
Pack instincts, 68, 214
Passive training, 142–145
Play training, 149–152
Playing, 147
Praise, 212–213
Protein, 57
Pulling, 153–154
Punishment, 155–156
Recall, 157–164
Rescued dogs, 175
Retrieving, 165–169
Reward training, 170–172
Road crossing, 55–56
Roaming, 173
Rolling in muck, 174
Scraps, feeding, 96
Second home, 175–177

Senses, 198–201
Sexual frustration, 237–238
Shaping, 178, 192
Showing, 181–185
Sit command, 186–188
Sleeping quarters, 29–30
Slip collars, 85
Socialisation, 99, 176, 190-192
Spaying, 136–137, 138
Speak on command, 103, 193-194
Stealing, 206–9
Stress, 23, 76
Submission, 71
Submissive behaviour, 204, 240
Submissive postures, 195
Submissiveness, 195–197
Supersense, 198–201
Tail chasing, 202
Tail wagging, 203–205
Teaching methods, 206
Thieving, 208
Thinking, 12, 170, 217
Timing, 167, 170, 210, 212-213, 221-223, 244
Toys, 86, 147, 159, 214-216
Training, 78, 217-223
Travel sickness, 224
Travelling, 224–226
Treats, 228–229
Tricks, 230–231
Triggers, 116, 142, 222-223, 232-233
Unpredictable behaviour, 234–235
Unusual behaviour, 237–238
Urinating indoors, 239–240
Urination, submissive, 196
Visitors, 241–242
Walking to heel, 154, 243-245
White, Michael, 7
Working dogs, 246–248
Working trials, 185
Worms, 23, 249
Young dogs, 250

EVERYBODY CAN
TRAIN
THEIR OWN DOG

THE ESSENTIALS OF DOG TRAINING